IMPOSSIBLE JOURNEYS

Mathew Lyons

CADOGAN

Published by Cadogan Guides 2005
Copyright © Mathew Lyons 2005

Cover design: Sarah Gardner

Cadogan Guides
2nd Floor, 233 High Holborn
London WC1V 7DN
info@cadoganguides.co.uk
www.cadoganguides.com

The Globe Pequot Press
246 Goose Lane, PO Box 480, Guilford,
Connecticut 06437–0480

Printed in Italy by Legoprint
A catalogue record for this book is available
from the British Library
ISBN 1-86011-333-8

For Helen
who makes everything possible

Contents

IMPOSSIBLE

JOURNEYS

Introduction

In which the author explains himself

The central idea of *Impossible Journeys* is this: what would the world look like if you could take a map and wipe it clean, and then start restoring to it all the impossible or lost destinations that have fallen off along the way? It is a book for those who, like me, are as least as much interested in what the world once contained – even if only in conjecture – as in what it actually contains today. It is also for those who half-regret the slow, empirical death by discovery of a world in which almost anything *was* possible because no one really knew what lay over the horizon.

What, though, constitutes an impossible journey? Once you stop to think about it, almost everything is impossible – the past being a foreign country and all that – and some criteria are required. The categories I have attempted to work within, then, are as follows:

— attempted journeys to places that did not in fact exist;

— claims to have visited or seen such places;

— journeys it is no longer possible to make; and

— journeys that, whether in the planning, the execution or the out-
come, were implausible or unlikely, if not actually wholly
impossible.

Clearly, these categories are still vast, and within them I have
given myself considerable latitude. My ultimate criterion, if truth be
told, was: did it interest or amuse me? On one level I asked myself if
the tale might change – even if only for the time it took to read – the
way we look out at the world. But, on another level, I was just thinking: is this going to be fun to read? The answer – I hope always –
should be yes. There is absurdity here, death, tenacity, greed, high
drama, vanity, courage and vision – and a dozen other qualities
besides. All, I think, offer small windows onto other versions of the
world.

Although each 'tale' stands on its own, many are to a greater or
lesser extent linked – through, for instance, the participants, their
intentions or their inspirations. Sometimes these are sequential: one
of the Lovers' Tales happened as a direct consequence of the Native's
Tale. Sometimes the connection is at more of a tangent: the
American sea-captain Benjamin Morrell appears in both the
Survivor's Tale and the Mapmakers' Tales, for instance. At a more
superficial level, there are many threads of fact and rumour, sometimes merely footnoted[1] and stray, that weave their way among
different tales, binding them, howsoever loosely, together.

It is probably inevitable that a good number of these stories concern the moment at which the New World rose over the horizon of
the known. It was, quite literally, a stunning discovery, dealing a
death blow to traditional geographical thinking, based as it was on
classical precedents. Even so, it was decades before everyone conced-
ed that the Americas actually *were* wholly new continents. Nearly a

---

1. There are a *lot* of footnotes, for which I make no apologies. If ever a book required
tangents and digressions, it is this one; after all, it is itself a collection of cartographical
or historical *cul de sacs*.

century after Columbus, the Elizabethan sailor and explorer Sir Martin Frobisher could still sail up the Hudson Strait believing that he was passing between America to the south and Asia to the north.

But if America were possible, what else might be? If rumour and hearsay had always been on a slack leash on the quaysides of Europe, from the days of Herodotus onwards, the discovery of the New World found them running wild. This whole book is, in some ways, a tribute to the power of such things: to the ability to spin talk out of imagination and belief. François Rabelais, the great French satirist, writing in the late 1540s in the wake of his country's Saguenay debacle,[2] could in *Gargantua and Pantagruel* mock those who attended the school of Hearsay, 'a diminutive, monstrous, misshapen old fellow', in the land of Satin,[3] among them the aforementioned Herodotus, but also Solinus, Cartier[4] and Polo – all of whom can be met, even if only fleetingly in some cases, in these pages – 'and forty cartloads of other modern historians, lurking behind a piece of tapestry, where they were at it ding-dong, privately scribbling the Lord knows what, and making rare work of it; and all by Hearsay'.

I, however, have taken the opposite approach. In so doing, I have tried to ensure, as best I can, that *Impossible Journeys* is not a book of fictions. Pure fantasy has been excluded; everything, I felt, required some kind of purchase on reality, however tenuous. These are all, perhaps perversely, true stories: everything actually happened, or at least was genuinely claimed or believed to have happened. There is one anomaly – a conscious fiction later believed to be true – but you will have to discover that for yourself.

The truth is that the relationship between travel and fiction in the age of exploration is subtle, complex and full of mutual distrust. Each side of the divide reflected doubt and faith back across to the other in about equal measure. They were bound together in a kind of dependency – not least by hearsay – but were in denial about the fact. Travellers were, say, happy to despise the great but almost certainly

2. See the Native's Tale.
3. Ironically, a real place: see the Legate's Tale.
4. It was once thought that Rabelais had been friends with Cartier, staying at his house and even drafting the accounts of his three voyages on which the Native's Tale is based.

fictional fabulist Sir John Mandeville, when it suited them; but always there seems to have lurked the possibility that his 'fables' were true. Frobisher took Mandeville's book to Meta Incognita in 1576. Richard Hakluyt printed them in his groundbreaking work *The Principall Navigations, Voiages and Discoveries of the English Nation* (first published in 1589 and hereafter referred to as simply *Voyages and Discoveries*). Raleigh wondered out loud whether his tales might, after all, be matter-of-fact. Marco Polo may not now be considered a fantasist in the Mandeville mould, but, for centuries afterwards, the same cloud of suspicion enveloped them all, as Rabelais shows.

Writers, for their part, were happy to use the discoveries and the sense of the unknown to spice up their work. It was a convenient and more or less infinite resource from which to mine sententious proverbial insights and high rhetoric. Thus, the fashionable John Lyly could write easily and glibly in 1580 of wisdom 'Whose rare qualities caused so strange events, that the wise were allured to vanity and the wantons to virtue, much like the river in Arabia, which turneth gold to dross, and dirt to silver' – or 'I see that India bringeth gold, but England breedeth goodness'. They used it as they used classical mythology, for the most part without much concern for the factual truth of what they wrote. Shakespeare could throw in references to the aphrodisiac qualities of potatoes – 'let the sky rain potatoes,' says Falstaff, waiting for his mistress in *The Merry Wives of Windsor* – or sun-worshiping natives, as Berowne to Rosaline in *Love's Labours Lost*: 'Vouchsafe to show the sunshine of your face/That we, like savages, may worship it' – without worrying that his audience would question them. As with the mapmakers filling the margins of their maps with sea-monsters, griffins and the like, or inventing coastlines that no man had seen,[5] the blankness invited invention.

Some writers, it's true, did make the effort to be accurate. It has been shown, for instance, that Marlowe, in writing *Tamburlaine the Great* – which would so entrance Thomas Coryat that he claimed

5. See the Mapmakers' Tales.

that he walked all the way to India to ask the Great Mogul's permission to view Tamerlane's tomb[6] – tried to be as scrupulous as possible in his use of geography. Specifically, it has been argued that as he wrote he must have had open a copy of Abraham Ortelius's *Theatrum Orbis Terrarum* (1570), the first world atlas. The routes of the armies – and there are a lot of them – can all be traced from place names in Ortelius and, ironically, Marlowe's error in placing Zanzibar actually in eastern Africa, and not as an island off its coast, is not in fact his own.

If you couldn't trust the mapmakers, who could you trust? Clearly not the seamen, who were responsible for much of the fantastical hearsay in the first place. We see them here and there in the background, in the words of Thomas Nashe,

> these swaggering captains (that wore a whole ancient in a scarf, which made them go heave shouldered, it was so boisterous) or huftytufty youthful ruffling comrades, wearing every one three yards of feather in his cap for his mistress's favour, such as we stumble on at every second step at Plymouth, Southampton and Portsmouth.

George Chapman, Ben Jonson and John Marston had a go at satirizing them in their play *Eastward Ho!* (1603), in the figure of Captain Seagull, who tells his audience in the Blue Anchor Tavern at Billingsgate:

> I tell thee, gold is more plentiful there than copper is with us; and for as much red copper as I can bring, I'll have thrice the weight in gold. Why man, all their dripping pans and their chamber pots are pure gold; all the chains with which they chain up their streets are massy gold; all the prisoners they

6. See the Walker's Tale. There are various spellings of Tamerlane's name in use. The most authentic is Timur, but I have gone for Tamerlane throughout, which is the closest contemporary analogue to the way he was known by Marlowe and Coryat alike – Tamburlaine.

take are fettered in gold; and for rubies and diamonds they go forth on holidays and gather 'em by the seashore to hang on their children's coats, and stick in their caps.

But it is hard to satirize the already absurd, and compared to the tall tales of David Ingram – which Elizabeth's government took for fact – this was small beer.[7]

Who, then, are my forebears in this venture? There is, perhaps, Richard Hakluyt, the aforementioned Elizabethan scholar whose *Voyages and Discoveries* is the first great and more or less authoritative collection of trading and exploration narratives, without whose work this book would certainly be very different.[8] Yet he would hardly be pleased with the uses to which I have put his labours, pulling out, no doubt, the parts of which he was least proud, whether that's his riding 200 miles to hear a story about cannibalism[9] or Ingram's drunken fantasies, which Hakluyt sensibly dropped after the first edition. I probably have more in common with Hakluyt's less fussy successor, Samuel Purchas.

Or are my forebears the crews under sail, the captains staring sternly out at the horizon? Well, yes, perhaps. Yet also – and frankly, more plausibly – the inquisitive, even nosy, scribe at the quayside, pen at the ready – part cynic, part wide-eyed gull – listening to the sailors' tales, busily noting the latest rumour brought in fresh on the morning tide...

Looking over the stories here collected, I suspect that there were three principal classes of motivation. The first, of course, was money. For those earlier travellers heading east to Cathay and elsewhere, the riches weren't fabled, they were as real as the power and magnificence of the Khans and Moguls they encountered. So much so that

7. See the Drunkard's Tale.
8. It's nice to find Thomas Nashe, in his mock-encomium to his home town of Great Yarmouth, *Lenten Stuff* (1599), poring over Hakluyt: 'I mused how Yarmouth should be invested in such plenty and opulence, considering that in Mr Hakluyt's English Discoveries I have not come in ken of one mizzen mast of a man of war bound for the Indies or Mediterranean stern-bearer sent from her zenith or meridian.'
9. See the Cannibal's Tale.

for centuries after the discovery of the Americas many seamen – most notably the British in search of the elusive Northwest Passage which was believed to run over the top of the continent from the Atlantic to the Pacific – were still primarily motivated by the idea of the Americas as an obstacle on the westward route to China and the Indies. Then, of course, the manner in which Pizarro and Cortés had stumbled upon the extraordinary wealth of the Inca and Aztec empires sent hundreds of would-be conquistadors scurrying the length and breadth of Central and South America in search of the quick fix of riches. The Europeans, after all, weren't necessarily inter-ested in mining the stuff: they wanted it good to go. Sir Walter Raleigh didn't even take any mining or assaying tools when he made his move on El Dorado: he was expecting to pick the stuff up off the ground.[10] Although not as extreme, we might also include those who sought wealth from trade, such as Jackman and Pet on their way to Moscow, or Pegolotti, with his eccentric version of the silk route.[11]

The second type of motivation might be termed the paradise syn-drome. This includes, of course, stories of those who came close to the actual Earthly Paradise from which man – at least Judaeo-Christian man – had been banished.[12] It might also include those who discovered versions of paradise on their travels, whether in Damascus, Canada or, yet more prosaically, the Fens of eastern England.[13]

Then there was the lure of fame and, beyond that, a kind of immortality. It is the same imperative that makes the naming of names such an attractive and pleasurable activity – though few did it with the verve of Luke Foxe.[14] That kind of power is, of course, what pushes men to error and untruths, but it is also what makes them endure. John Ross and William Shepherd are hardly household names,[15] but they have survived into the historical record, where few

---

10. See the Courtier's Tale.
11. See the Apprentice's Tale and the Merchant's Tale, respectively.
12. See the Orientalists' Tales.
13. See the Grivy's Tale.
14. See the Survivor's Tale.
15. See the Officers' Tales and the Sea Captain's Tale, respectively.

of their contemporaries have joined them. Thomas Coryat, according to one friend, was entirely driven by 'the itch of fame'.

There is a short story by Kipling, called 'The Wandering Jew', that captures something of this kind of obsessive attraction, and the intoxicating sense of detachment and timelessness that travel – surely the most ephemeral of human cultural activities – can bring. In it a wealthy young man named John Hay is haunted by the idea that by travelling eastwards around the world he can gain a day. He comes to believe that that extra day will be a day won from death, so that:

> His days were divided between watching the white wake
> spinning behind the stern of the swiftest steamers, or the
> brown earth flashing past the windows of the fastest trains;
> and he noted in a pocket-book every minute that he had
> railed or screwed out of remorseless eternity.

He says to himself: 'This is better than praying for long life.'

Then something better yet finds him: a new idea. The story leaves him in a small, white house by the surf at Madras – perhaps close by the site of Marignolli's pillar, 'intended to last until the world's end'[16] – suspended in a chair that hangs from the roof, a steel sheet beneath to repel 'the attraction of the earth', swinging free, 'the equal of the undying sun', his face turned always towards the east where the sun itself rises, a stopwatch in his hand, in defiance of the ever-passing shadows.

It should perhaps be added that shadowing *Impossible Journeys*, and hidden within the category of 'journeys it is no longer possible to make', is another book – of impossible, if not infinite size – covering all the destinations that cannot be reached because they are gone: the buildings burned, destroyed or ruined; the lost streets of towns and cities buried beneath today's; the cities themselves disused and obscured now beneath earth, sea or sand. Faced square on, that would have been a book based wholly on the premise of the past as a another country from which we have been permanently banished, on

16. See the Legate's Tale.

the impossibility of going back. Since its remit could have covered the whole of human history – saving only that infinitesimal fraction that has been preserved – it would have been something of an ambitious undertaking.

Yet glimpses of that other book can still be had, if you care to look through to the other side of the various narratives. Much of the pleasure of Coryat's company, for instance, comes from the freshness of his observation of the now vanished world around him; people just didn't write like that then, not least because, Coryat excepted again, they didn't travel like that either. Then there are the lost cities of Pegolotti's journey to Beijing; or the Elizabethan royal manor at Dartford, the outer walls of which were built from Frobisher's ore; or Durham House, on the Strand, where Raleigh planned his first expedition to Guiana; or Hochelaga and Stadacona, buried beneath today's Montreal and Quebec City respectively.

One final point: in cleaving to fact, I can't promise that I have stripped away all the fictions. However, I hope that the reader will offer me some latitude if he or she encounters in what follows any errors, misstatements, exaggerations or downright untruths. Where they exist, they are unintentional; but they are also, I feel, firmly in the right tradition.

I have detained you long enough. Where should the book begin? Where it must: on a quayside, one bright morning...

The
Walker's
Tale

Thomas Coryat of Odcombe in Somerset
walks from England to India

homas Coryat stood by the harbour in Dover. It was 10 o'clock in the morning on 14 May 1608, a Saturday and the day before Whitsun. No doubt the talk of the town around him was the next day's May games and morris dances, and the other sports that the feast day promised. His mind would have been on other things, however. At 31, he had finally found his purpose in life. It was travel.

The son of the rector in the small village of Odcombe, near Yeovil, in Somerset, Coryat had always been something of a drifter. He had studied at Oxford, but, despite being endowed with a prodigious memory, he had failed to gain his degree. After university he had been sucked into the orbit of the royal court, joining the household of Henry, Prince of Wales, where he soon got a reputation as something of a buffoon. Yet he was no fool, as some had found to their cost: one contemporary recollection of him is as 'the courtiers' anvil to try their wits upon; and sometimes this anvil returned the hammers as hard knocks as it received, his bluntness repaying their abusiveness'.

Perhaps Coryat was happy with his station; possibly he felt he could aspire to little better. No portrait of him exists, but, in an age that was not squeamish about ridiculing the unsightly or grotesque, his features were considered peculiar enough to be a great source of amusement: 'The shape of his head had no promising form, being like a sugar loaf inverted, with the little end before, as composed of fancy and memory, without any common sense.'

There is, however, a pen portrait of him by Ben Jonson, who was a good friend. At court, Coryat was independent and independent-minded: he 'served in his own clothes and at his own costs,' says Jonson, and was as happy talking to the King's son-in-law as to the staff. Indeed, talk was the element Coryat lived in: he talked so much that he often forgot to eat – 'it is feared his belly will exhibit a bill in Chancery against his mouth for talking away his meals' – but this was out of generosity of spirit, not solipsism. 'He is frequent at all sorts of free tables, where though he might sit as the guest, he will rather be served in as a dish, and is loath to have any thing of himself kept cold against the next day.' It was said that feasts at court were finished off with sweetmeats and Coryat.

More than anything, Coryat sounds companionable, fun, his talk being spiced with 'phrases such as if they were studied to make mourners merry'. He was, too, interested in everything anyone had to say: 'He will ask, how you do?, where you have been?, how is it?, if you have travelled?, how you like his book?, with, what news? And be guilty of a thousand such courteous impertinences in an hour rather than want the humanity of vexing you.' It was for such qualities, no doubt, that he was made welcome by the famous coterie that frequented the Mermaid Tavern in Bread

Street on the first Friday of every month, and that seems to have included Jonson, John Donne, Inigo Jones and Samuel Purchas, among others.[1]

Above all, Coryat *was* obsessed with travel:

> The word travel affects him like a waine-ox or a pack-horse. A carrier will carry him from any company that hath not been abroad… a Dutch post doth ravish him. The mere superscription of a letter from Zurich sets him up like a top, Basle or Heidelberg make him spin. And at seeing the word Frankfurt or Venice, though but on the title of a book, he is ready to break doublet, crack elbows and overflow the room with his murmur.

That is what brought Coryat to Dover that fresh May morning. He had an idea, and it was, for its time, a startling one: he would travel abroad, not for profit, nor for the glory of discovery or conquest, but simply for the pleasure of the journey. For this reason he is, arguably, the first true travel writer ('none of these cities has been described in our language that I could ever hear of,' he later wrote). He wanted to see the world and, broadly, he wanted to see it alone. Few of us, however, would regard the goals he set himself as innately pleasurable. Ahead of him lay ten years and over 3,500 miles of travel; most of those miles would be on foot, at a time when Sir Francis Bacon could grumble that maps like Mercator's were all very well, but they didn't help him much in trying to find his way from York to London.

It was, on the face of it, an absurd objective, but Coryat courted ridicule and in some ways relished it: 'to that gayle he sets up all sails,' Jonson says. Yet, leaving aside the daunting scale of the challenge for

1. Sadly, the tradition, which dates from a few decades after the event, that the Friday Club also included Shakespeare and Raleigh is impossible to prove. Leaving aside the inherent implausibility that someone of Raleigh's self-importance and social status would hob-nob with impecunious gentlemen in any kind of public tavern, there is the added difficulty that he was imprisoned in the Tower of London for the entire period during which the club is known to have been active.

a man who, as far as we know, had never set foot outside England before, there were of course grave dangers. As a lone traveller, without the security that money can buy, he was ridiculously exposed. More than that, as an English Protestant he would have to cross Catholic Europe – in a very real sense enemy territory – before arriving at the greater unknowns that would lie in the Ottoman empire and beyond. These, at least, would come later. To begin with, his ambitions were somewhat more modest: he would simply walk to Venice and back.

Coryat seems to have been aware of the absurdity, at least, or his own personal absurdity in such a situation. It is hard to see why else he did not get beyond the first paragraph of his book[2] before telling his readers that he was seasick on the seven-hour crossing to Calais – or, as he refers to it, 'varnishing the exterior parts of the ship with the excremental ebullitions of my tumultuous stomach'. This is the comment and the turn of phrase of a man unsure of his audience and his material: keeping it broad, playing it for laughs.

In the first stages of his journey Coryat was unsure what to note. His comments and observations regarding Boulogne, Montrueil, Abbeville and the rest have a stiffness and formality about them that will soon appear uncharacteristic. But then, no one had ever done anything quite like this before, at least not in English. Perhaps Camden's groundbreaking *Britannia* (1586) was a model – a county-by-county Latin exploration of Britain, its history, geography and antiquarian remains. It was published while Camden was still a master at Westminster School; Jonson had been a pupil of his.[3] Yet Camden's intent was didactic, proselytizing: he wanted to prove the greatness of the nation. Coryat, in contrast, was an entertainer first. He wished to delight. Yet he was no less innovative for all that:

2. Its splendid full title is *Coryat's Crudities hastily gobbled up in five months travells in France, Savoy, Italy, Rhetia commonly called the Grisons country, Helvetia alias Switzerland, & some parts of high Germany, and the Netherlands; newly digested in the hungry aire of Odcombe in the county of Somerset, & now dispersed to the nourishment of the travelling members of this kingdom.*

3. It was a small world. In later life, Camden, Coryat, Raleigh and Jonson all shared the same printer, William Stansby. Coryat and Camden also shared the same illustrator.

travel as entertainment is so familiar an idea to us that it can take some effort to imagine a time when, unless you were very wealthy, it was something merely to be endured, if not avoided altogether.

By the time Coryat reached Paris on Friday 20 May, however, he had relaxed and, one might say, found himself. Perhaps it took a major city to do that. He had begun to reach towards, if not a formula, then at least some kind of working practice. Perhaps one shouldn't be surprised by the familiarity of it, since the travel shelves of every bookshop and library are filled with the writings of those who have, probably unknowingly, followed in his footsteps. He sees the sights; he comments on quirky customs; he reports on big events, if he has chanced to see them; he mixes in a bit of history; he leaves. Reduced to a bald summary like that, it all sounds eminently 'so what?'-ish. Yet, as will become apparent, what drew Coryat's eye was not – especially as he grew older – the stuff of everyday guides, even by today's quirky liberal standards.

Then, of course, even the straight travelogue he offers is a constant surprise because so much of what he describes has been lost. Indeed, Coryat supplies what is missing from most writing before the modern era, and what histories – thanks to the general paucity of material – always struggle to colour in: an everyday sense of place. He sees things as they are, not – as most of his contemporaries would – as figurative tropes: mountains are mountains in Coryat, not metaphors. In this sense he belongs to the modern world more than to his own.[4]

It was the 'fair white stone' of Paris that caught his eye first. It was everywhere, he thought; he had never seen a city so bright and uni-

---

4. You have only to compare him to slightly earlier writers to see how different Coryat is. Thomas Nashe's *Unfortunate Traveller* (1594) is a candidate for being among the first English novels. Set in the reign of Henry VIII, it tells of the adventures of one Jack Wilton across Europe. The locations are incidental and Nashe is, in any case, indifferent to them. In Rome he throws in a few buildings just to show willing – 'I was at Pontius Pilate's house and pissed against it,' being the most memorable quotation – and then excuses himself from the effort: 'These are but the shop-dust of the sights that I saw, and in truth I did not behold with any care hereafter to report, but contented my eye for the present, and so let them pass.' Besides, he adds, it's frivolous to detail too many sights, 'since he that hath but once drunk with a traveller talks of them.' Nashe and Coryat are

form. Coming from ramshackle old London, he was particularly impressed by the Rue de la Notre Dame, where the buildings were almost identical in quality and style. He visited the Louvre, then a small royal palace, and gazed up in awe at timbered ceilings gilded with such craft and guile that they looked like beaten gold. This was in the room he calls the Presence, the grand chamber in which the French King met his subjects. Next came the Queen's chamber – the Queen in question being the formidable Marie de Medici – where a rail surrounded the bed area, supported by pretty gilt pillars. Passing through it Coryat came next to a room, which, ill-advisedly, he said 'excelleth in my opinion, not only all those that are now in the world, but also all whatsoever that ever there were since the creation...' He was given to overexcited hyperbole, but launching into such a vast superlative with his toe just dipped into continental waters was somewhat rash. There was Venice still to come, and Constantinople...

Not that the room was lacking, being some 500 paces long and 10 paces wide. (Coryat liked measuring things, pacing them out.) The walls, he reckoned, were two yards thick. The gallery itself was divided into three parts, two 'sides' flanking a spacious walk in the middle. Pictures of French kings and queens were carved into the woodwork and overpainted with oils, an effect that Coryat admired. The ceiling drew his attention again: it was 'of most glittering and admirable beauty', with God and his angels, the sun, the moon, the stars and planets pictured thereon. At the far end the great doors were offset by pillars of flesh-coloured marble, veined with white; there was much blue slate.

---

thus hardly simpatico. Elsewhere in *The Unfortunate Traveller* Nashe asks, 'what is here but we may read in books, and a great deal more too, without stirring our feet out of a warm study?' That was not exactly Coryat's point of view. Yet Nashe is a veritable Baedeker compared to John Lyly. In his hugely successful *Euphues and his England* (1580), for instance, Lyly's eponymous Italian hero decants to London. Despite the fact that almost all the action of the book takes place there, you would be hard-pressed to glean even the slightest information about the city from its pages. London has a court, a gentleman's house and a merchant's house – and that is the barest minimum to get the plot, such as it is, going.

Then we discover further evidence of Coryat's over-enthusiasm, for the room was somewhat more lacking than he had led us to believe: it was, in fact, unfinished. Fully half of the walk remained unboarded and the roof, too, was incomplete. The windows were half-done, the partitions not a quarter. Coryat counted 200 masons working every day to finish off the work. For the reader, though, this is good: we are used to our heritage being static, as if set in amber. It is refreshing to encounter it, as we do here, unmade, merely in the process of becoming.

There is a similar story in the garden of the nearby Palace of the Tuileries, which would be burned down by the Communards in 1871. Coryat admired a great fountain, even as he observed its lack of water and fish, and watched the workmen laying lead piping. Naturally, this being Coryat, it was the 'fairest garden he has ever seen'. (One begins to suspect that he couldn't have got out much in London. Either that, or London really had very little to hold a candle to continental Europe. Perhaps the latter is closer to the truth; about the only architectural comparison Coryat makes in which England comes off better is between the playhouses of London and Venice.) Clearly, though, Coryat was a sucker for things on a grand scale. There were two great walks in the garden, he reported, each 700 paces long; one was of particular beauty, with maple boughs trained to arch above the path and six arbours along its length, like turrets. Coryat had, in his own estimation at least, a good ear for music: at the end of the garden was an echoing grove, where he was enchanted by a man singing melodiously 'with curious quavers' and 'with such art it sounded like three men'.

Out on the streets Coryat was surprised to see even the greatest of men riding on mules rather than horses. He was less surprised to visit Notre Dame for the feast of Corpus Christi and find the pomp and ceremony of the Catholic Church very much not to his taste. Indeed, so strong is his aversion that one half feels that he protests too much. He attended 'for novelty's sake,' he said, 'not for any hearty devotion. I was content to behold, as being the first that ever I saw of that kind and I heartily wish they may be the last.' It may be that he did feel genuine revulsion; the feast is not celebrated in Protestant churches since it centres on the real presence of Christ in the Eucharist. On the other hand, he perhaps thought it politic to set out some Protestant credentials right at the start, lest anyone think that, as other young men did, he was travelling in Europe with the aim of reverting to the 'old faith'.

At Fontainebleau, to the south of Paris, Coryat seems to have passed swiftly through the gardens. He admired the fountains, where stone dolphins spewed out water, and he noted the pools full of carp and the mossy artificial rocks, but he was rather more interested in something he hasn't seen before – shutters:

> In the inside of the room, [the window] hath timber leaves, joined together with certain little iron bolts, which being loosed, and the leaves opened, there cometh in at the lower part of the window where there is no glass at all, the open air very pleasantly. The upper part of the window, which is most commonly shut, is made of glass or lattice.

Coryat moved quickly southwards, riding post from Fontainebleau and passing the Loire Valley, Nevers and Moulins in short order. On 3 June he was in Lyons, the city where, as he noted speculatively, if with grim satisfaction, Pontius Pilate was said to have committed suicide. Another striking observation: the windows here were mostly made of white paper, some wholly so, others with paper at the bottom but glass on top. Unusually, Coryat also tells us where he stayed, a sure sign that he is proud of it. He was at the sign of the Three Kings, 'the fairest inn in the whole city,' he reports, and here we glimpse a sense of the lure that Coryat clearly felt for men of wealth and status, and which was no doubt the reason he had borne the taunts and jests of so many back at court. The Three Kings, he lets us know, is the busiest inn in Lyons, and the most visited by 'great persons'. The Earl of Essex and his entourage had been there for the best part of a week, leaving the day before Coryat arrived. He leaves gently hanging the implication that the Earl would have been as disappointed to miss Coryat as Coryat was to miss him.

Coryat was, however, sharing the inn with a brother of Charles de Lorraine, the fourth Duke of Guise. Coryat listened to the fine music that was played at supper, and watched the nobleman's men dancing 'chorantos' and 'lavoltas' in the courtyard. Something else caught Coryat's roving eye, too:

> On the south side of the wall of another court, there was a very pretty and merry story painted, which was this: a certain pedlar having a [bag] full of small wares, fell asleep as he was travelling along the way, to whom there came a great multitude of apes, and robbed him of all his wares while he was asleep. Some of those apes were painted with pouches or [bags] at their backs, which they stole out of the pedlar's fardle, climbing up to trees – some with spectacles on their noses, some with beads about their necks, some with touch boxes and inkhorns in their hands, some with crosses and censor boxes, some with cards in their hands (all things which they stole out of the [bag]). And among the rest, one putting down the pedlar's breeches and kissing his naked etc.[5]

And this, let's not forget, was on the wall of the best inn in the city. One wonders what the lower-class establishments might have had to offer. Coryat suddenly turns coy, in any case: 'This pretty conceit seemeth to import some merry matter, but truly I know not the moral of it,' he writes.

In Lyons Coryat also had to get a certificate confirming his state of health, since the authorities of the major Italian states wouldn't admit strangers into their cities without such a confirmation that they were 'free from all manner of contagious sickness'. The Venetians were particularly tough on this score, as Coryat notes somewhat disapprovingly: 'The Venetians are extraordinarily precise herein, insomuch that a man cannot be received into Venice without a bill of health, if he would give a thousand ducats.' The idea that money couldn't buy better access seemed ridiculously naive.

Moving southeastwards from Lyons, Coryat was heading towards Piedmont (also known as Savoy, after its ruling family) a kingdom

---

5. Readers can make their own decisions as to what precisely this 'etc.' refers to.

straddling the Alps that, despite centuries of best French efforts to absorb it, survived until 1860, to become the nucleus of unified Italy (while losing Nice and some other cities to France). Coryat had left Lyons early in the afternoon of 6 June and was at the border by the following evening, admiring the walnut groves he had ridden through.

Coryat could see the Alps up ahead. He was interested in the abundant red snails; the chestnut trees, which helped to feed the local black pigs; the barley already ripe in the fields some two months ahead of the English harvest. The quantity of the vineyards amazed him: 'for the space of ten whole miles together a man could not perceive any vacant or waste place under the Alps', he says. Looking up into the mountains, he noticed the wooden tiles on the houses, which he had not encountered before, as well as the fine green meadows and the many small cornfield plots endlessly clustered beneath the tops of the mountains.

This was Coryat's first encounter with mountains, and it was an uncomfortable experience for him. The road led from Chambery – until the 1560s actually the capital of Savoy, before it was transferred to Turin – to Aiguebelette. Coryat wished to go up on foot, but the companions he was travelling with had other ideas. They employed some local men to carry them up in chairs, one at the front and one at the back, the chair supported by two poles borne on the poor men's shoulders. Coryat, though, was shocked by their poverty and the desperation that it bred. Such was their need that they found his insistence on walking infuriating. They raced ahead up twisting winding paths, set deep among the dense woods, determined to make the climb impossible for him without their assistance, and Coryat found it miserably painful to keep up.

The roads themselves were as bad as the worst English roads in midwinter, he thought. Still, there were always the Alps to look at: the torrents of melted water cascading down; the snowy peaks and the pine trees high up towards the skyline; the goats leaping carelessly among the olive trees, the beeches and the hazels. And it is interesting to note in passing that here Coryat is racking up another first for himself. This marks the first meaningful appearance in the

English imagination of the Alps – which would so inspire, absorb and overwhelm the Romantics when they 'discovered' the mountain range for themselves nearly 200 years later. Arguably, Coryat, less in awe of nature, offers the better account.

In any event, it is at this point that we discover, if we hadn't guessed already, that Coryat was a careful, not to say a nervous man. The mountain paths led them alongside some terrifying drops – some as deep, he says, as St Paul's is high.[6] Coryat dismounted, so as to prevent any catastrophe, and continued on foot; his companions, oblivious to his concerns, rode on as they were.

By now there is a growing intimacy to the tone and subject matter. Staying at a village in the Alps, Coryat reports the beds to be 'so high that a man could hardly get into his bed without some kind of climbing'. He was unimpressed by the fact that the women of the region 'gird themselves so high that the distance between their shoulders and their girdle seems to be but a little handful'. There were great swarms of butterflies in the air, thousands of them dead upon the road; above him, the highest Alpine peaks were lost in cloud, as if in their own weather system.

Coming down into Italy, Coryat again found the mountain paths nerve-racking:

I was constrained to walk afoot for the space of seven miles, for so much it is betwixt the top and the foot of the mountain, in all which space I continually descended headlong. The wayes were exceeding uneasy. For they were wonderful hard all stony and full of windings and intricate turnings, whereof I think there were at least 20 hundred before I came to the foot.

Once in Italy, which they crossed into on 11 June, Coryat was aggrieved – as he always was when money was lost – that the party

---

6. Churches are the only real comparators that writers of the period had for natural phenomena of any size. Thus, where Coryat compares chasms to them, Raleigh does the same with waterfalls and Frobisher with icebergs.

was searched by the local officials in Susa and their money confiscated. Still, he was not so put out that he couldn't admire the straw hats worn by the Piedmontese, men and women alike. Those worn by the latter, in particular, were very pretty: some seemed to have a hundred seams of silk, woven with silver, and floral borders and branches all beautifully wrought. Meanwhile, the travellers were entertained by one of their number, named Antonio, who claimed to be descended from Marc Antony; on the journey down from the Alps he 'would oftentimes cheer us with this sociable conceit: "*Courage, courage, le Diable est mort*" – be merry, for the Devil is dead'.

It is the details that bring Coryat's travels alive: the oxen in Lombardy, pulling carts, white linen pegged over them to ward off flies; young children with no backs to their breeches in the summer heat; the white canopies that adorned so many inns, pointed with needlework and lace. In Milan he spends much of his one day there – Wednesday 15 June, to be precise – admiring the cutlers' art, the embroidery on the swords and daggers, the exquisite hilts. In Padua the Benedictine monastery could show off two crocodile skins that were worth a visit, the sort of strange and monstrous prodigies that the English had little access to.

For the most part, though, Coryat's sojourn in the cities of northern Italy was uneventful. In Turin he fell ill from the after-effects of too much sweet wine in Piedmont: his hands and face swelled up badly and he resolved to drink no more wine unless it was mixed with water – a pledge that he would later fail to adhere to, with tragic consequences. More petulantly, he was unhappy with what he regarded as the baffling and unnecessary Italian habit of lading cheese over so much of their food:

> I observed a custom in many towns and cities of Italy which
> did not a little displease me, that most of their best meats
> which come to the table are sprinkled with cheese, which I
> love not so well as the Welshmen do, whereby I was
> oftentimes constrained to lose my share of much good fare to
> my great discontentment...

One habit he did pick up, however, has transformed English eating habits – the use of the fork:

> I observed a custom that is not used in any other country that I saw in my travels, neither do I think that any other country in Christendom doth use it, but only Italy. The Italian and also most strangers that are cormorant in Italy do always at their meals use a little fork when they cut their meat. For while with their knife which they hold in one hand they cut the meat out of the dish, they fasten their fork which they hold in their other hand upon the same dish, so that whatsoever he be that sitting in the company of any others at meal, should unadvisedly touch the dish of meat with his fingers from which all at the table do cut, he will give occasion of offence unto the company, in so much that for his error he shall be at the least browbeaten, if not reprehended in words... Hereupon I myself thought good to imitate the Italian fashion by this forked cutting of meat, not only while I was in Italy, but in Germany and oftentimes in England since I came home.

The triumph of Coryat's time in Italy, was, however, clearly Venice. He spent six weeks there, which were

> the sweetest time for so much that ever I spent in my life; partly because [Venice] ministered unto me more variety of delicious and remarkable objects than mine eyes ever surveyed in any city before, or ever shall, if I should with famous Sir John Mandeville our English Ulysses spend thirty whole years together in travelling over most places of the Christian and ethnic world.

Six weeks was a long time for Coryat. A later acquaintance described him as being 'like a perpetual motion'; he could pack a lot in. While he is diligent in his descriptions of the great churches and palaces of Venice, the bridges, the Rialto, and so on, it is the other things he has to say, the things glimpsed out of the corner of his eye, the asides, that arguably hold more interest, and certainly more charm. Here you can see the people of Venice, not too far off its peak as a city, as they were, strange customs, beliefs and ceremonies mingling with the everyday mundanities of life.

Coryat went everywhere, but we might begin by following him to what he calls the marketplace of St Mark's, the 'fairest place, of admirable and incomparable beauty that I think no place whatsoever, either in Christendom or Paganism may compare to it'. (Whether this makes it better than the unfinished gallery in the Louvre is a moot point.) Here, he says, twice a day – between 6 and 11 in the morning, and then between 5 and 8 in the evening – 'is the marketplace of the world, not a mere city'. All manner of fashions are here, and all the languages of Christendom can be heard, with 'many barbarous ethnic ones besides'. Here the people came to promenade, to walk about, being seen and seeing. When they met with acquaintances, he was shocked to see them kiss one another on the cheek, 'a custom that I never saw before nor heard nor read in any history'.

Whatever his view of social customs, Coryat liked the way that Venetian gentlemen, in particular, dressed, with clothes of red only beneath their long black gowns. They had a dignity and simplicity with which the English could not compete, he felt:

> Whereas they have but one colour we use many more than are in the rainbow, all the most light, garish, and unseemly colours that are in the world. Also for fashion we are much inferior to them, for we wear more fantastical fashions than any nation under the sun – the French only excepted – which hath given occasion both to the Venetian and other Italians to brand the Englishman with a notable mark of levity, by painting him stark naked with a pair of shears in his hand.

As for women's fashions, out on the Piazza San Marco or elsewhere, Coryat was more ambivalent. Women were mostly veiled, wives and widows in black, 'maids' in white or pale yellow. The veils, which might fall the length of their bodies, were of thin, slight silk, through which, he said, they might look out, and you might snatch a fleeting glimpse of their face as they slipped past. Almost all women walked 'with their breasts all naked… many of them [with] their backs also naked even almost to the middle, which some do cover with a slight linen…' Coryat was enough of a Puritan to disapprove strongly of this. It is, he says, 'a fashion methinks very uncivil and unseemly, especially if the beholder might plainly see them. For I believe they would minister a great incentive and fomentation of luxurious desires.'

For a man with more than a touch of Puritanism Coryat was surprisingly interested in, and informed about, women's fashions. He tells us about fans, 'elegant and pretty things', and evidently something of a novelty to him, and umbrellas, too – his being the first recorded use of the word in English – which 'minister shadow unto them for shelter against the scorching heat of the sun'.[7] He also tells us about 'chapineys', wooden undershoes, painted and sometimes gilded, which were a mark of social status: the bigger the chapiney, the nobler the lady. The biggest Coryat saw were about half a yard high: women would venture out with the support of a maid or a gentleman, always offered to the left arm only. He saw one woman, wearing them but unaccompanied, toppling over by the Rialto; he thought it rather funny.

Every Saturday Venetian women spent the afternoon bleaching their hair. Coryat knew this, because – unusually – he had been allowed to watch a Venetian woman while she went through the process. She put on a broad-brimmed but crownless hat and sat out in the sun, pulling her hair up over the brim. Then she dyed her hair with oils or unguents and sat waiting for it to dry. Finally, she 'curled it up in curious locks with a frisling or crisping pin of iron' so that the hair on each side of her forehead accumulated into a peak.

7. Given that umbrellas had been known and used in Italy for nearly 300 years by this time – see the Legate's Tale – it seems extraordinary that they were still unknown in England.

When he could drag his attention away from fashion, Coryat also found the mountebanks of Venice extremely amusing. For the most part they sold trifles – oils, waters, amorous songs – but it was the sales patter, sometimes two hours in the telling, that he revelled in, the extempore songs, the scurrilous – if not downright filthy – tales. He doesn't quite say so, but it would be surprising if he were not a good friend to them; he certainly seems a touch credulous about it all. He was amazed that, however high the price they started with, they were always happy to settle for pence. He was astounded to see one man playing with a viper. Another appeared to gash his arm with a knife, the blood streaming from the wound, to Coryat's horror; but on the application of an ointment, the wound miraculously closed, without even the merest scar.

There's no doubt that Venice had Coryat wholly in its thrall. When he climbed the tower of St Mark's he even admired the way the Venetians cut their stairs. At the top of the tower he felt on top of the world. In the far distance, he says, he could see the Alps, but below him, laid out like a map, was the city – 'the Jerusalem of Christianity' – its squares and steeples, its monasteries and islands, and its gardens, where oranges, lemons and apricots grew.

Coryat dwells here more on food and drink than he does at any other destination. Partly, one suspects, that is just because of the sheer abundance of both: 'Amongst many other things that moved great admiration in me in Venice, this was not the least, to consider the marvellous affluence and exuberancy of all things tending to the sustentation of man's life.' We see him picking out the best black figs, or supping on green-lipped oysters in the gardens of Murano where the glassblowers worked, or surfeiting on 'one of the most delectable dishes for a summer fruit of all Christendom, namely musk melons'. For a month in summer, he says, the markets overflowed with them, and he must have eaten too many of his favourite red ones, since he advises the reader 'to abstain from the immoderate eating of them'. Yet, for all that, he is not impressed that the greatest of men in the city – those worth two million ducats or more, he reckons – come down to the markets in person each day to buy their meat, fish, fruit and any other things their families required. He thought it beneath their dignity.

Away from the markets and piazzas, we glimpse Coryat everywhere among the Venetians. He fell out with the gondoliers who waited for the ferry under the Rialto Bridge. They were, he said, 'the most vicious and licentious varlets about all in the City. For if a stranger enters one of their gondolas and does not presently tell them where he will go, they will incontinently carry him of their own accord to a religious house forsooth, where his plumes will be well pulled before he comes forth again.'

He went to the Arsenal, at the east end of the city, admiring the world's first production line. Some 1,500 men worked here all the time and when they were too old to work they received pensions from the state. So big was the Arsenal that there are always 250 galleys there, with another 50 out at sea. He saw the vast golden galley, the *Bucentoro*, big enough to hold 1,220 men, with the golden throne from which the Doge cast out the ring with which he wedded the sea on Ascension Day.

He went, too, to the playhouse, marvelling at seeing women on stage for the first time and finding them to have 'as good a grace, action and gesture as ever I saw any masculine actor'. He also found himself looking up at the 'noble and famous courtesans', sitting alone in the best boxes available. Their faces were obscured by double masks and their necks were 'so covered and wrapped with cobweb lawn and other things that no part of their skin could be discerned'. They wore little black felt caps and short black taffeta cloaks. Coryat was told that if anyone tried to unmask them they would be cut to pieces.

One suspects that Coryat could have stayed in Venice to the end of his days, but he had to return to England. He had, as was then common practice, taken out an insurance policy when he left that would pay him fivefold just for returning home safe. He left on 8 August 1608.

When Coryat resumed his travels, on 20 August 1612, aiming this time for the court of the Great Mogul in distant India, he would become more elusive, harder to track down. The principal reason is that he never lived to write his planned companion volume to *Coryat's Crudities*. What we know of his travels from then on comes from a handful of letters – which only survive in their heavily edited published forms – and a few chance meetings along the way. Perhaps it is because what survives is fragmentary, but the further east Coryat walked, the more strange and outlandish – even dream-like – his experiences and reports seem to become.

In any event, Coryat emerges again on Zakinthos, one of the Ionian Islands to the west of the Peloponnese, where he arrived on 13 January 1613. Through most of the Middle Ages and the early modern period the island was better known to the outside world by its French name, Zante, despite the fact that from 1485 until 1797 it was held by the Venetians. The outside world knew it well: Zante was famed throughout the known world for its wine, oil and currants, which commanded high prices in the great markets, such as those of Constantinople and Aleppo.

On his later travels Coryat was more leisurely in his approach. Whereas previously he had spent no more than a few days, at most, at any given place – with the notable exception of Venice – now he was in no hurry to move anywhere. On Zante, where there was little civic grandeur to detain him, to put it mildly, he dawdled, fascinated with the low, flat-roofed houses built with stone dug from the mountain, with their glassless windows and latticework of fir. He saw local weddings, too, was amused by the custom of hanging carpets out of the windows and was shocked to see women riding astride donkeys, rather than side-saddle.

Coryat was also on Zante long enough to experience an earthquake for the first time, and the still sea that preceded it, the strange sense of quiet. He reported that Zante and its neighbour, Cephalonia, sometimes had as many as 10 shocks a month. They never lasted more than 15 minutes, however, and usually just two or three. Nevertheless, people were 'driven out of doors, even out of their naked beds, men in their shirts, women in their smocks, carrying up their clothes with them, that they have hastily caught up...' The people responded each time by ringing the cracked church bells and marching in procession about the castle, beseeching God to spare them. But then they were a religious people: the island contained, on Coryat's count, some 43 churches and chapels.

By 22 February Coryat was alighting from an English ship onto the shores of Anatolia. He and his companions were about to become the first Englishmen to visit the ruins of Troy.[8] There were 14 travellers in all: presumably the others were merchants, although Coryat doesn't say so. They had with them a Jew, acting as dragoman, or interpreter. All were well-armed and wary of the Turks, whose land this was and is.

They came first to the ruins of a fortress by the shore. Coryat reckoned that there were perhaps 100 marble pillars buried in the earth. The ground was rough and scabrous, with wheat and corn growing among the broken columns. Trees were scattered across the uneven land: mulberry, fig, box, olive, oak and almond. Coryat liked the great broom trees dotted here and there, their pretty scent mingling with the salt of the sea. In just one area, on a low plot of ground near the water, was the plain still smooth, 'like a sleeking stone'. Nearby were four or five sepulchres, fashioned out of whole blocks of white marble, some nine feet long. Each corner was rounded off with small curls of stone, 'like little pillows', and on the left-hand flank of each casket could still be seen two hands carved perfectly into the marble. Coryat was aggrieved that there were no inscriptions to identify the dead. Conjectures are vain, he said to himself. This didn't stop him guessing: one of them might, he thought, be the tomb of Priam, the last King of Troy.

The travellers walked on to the site of Troy itself, Coryat clearly struggling to transform what he could see into the glorious city of Homeric and Virgilian myth. He identified the harbour, now too shallow for ships to ride safe at anchor, where fallen pillars of grey marble were visible beneath the water. From there he climbed the steps from the sea – the 'still worthy steps of antiquity', he says, hopefully – towards what he believed was the royal palace, a mile from the water's edge. The steps were wide enough for three carts to pass along, but much broken and scattered. At the palace three white stone arches towered above the ruins, a large one flanked by two smaller.

8. At least, they thought that it was Troy. There's little way of knowing exactly where they were, although it is usually considered that Troy wasn't rediscovered until the 19th century (if then), through the brilliant work of the self-publicizing archaeologist and all-round rascal Heinrich Schliemann.

Coryat measured them: the whole piece was 40 feet wide and 36 feet high. Another column close by was 33 feet long. Yet, as he noted with evident regret, the grandeur and the 'beautiful grace of the stone [were] somewhat diminished by antiquity'. Aside from these, Priam's palace (as Coryat believed it to be) wasn't much more than broken stone and brick. Coryat worked himself up to a rare moral: 'You may also observe as in a clear looking glass one of the most pregnant examples of luxury that ever was in the world in these confused heaps of stones.'

Even somewhere as full of meaning as Troy couldn't stop Coryat from being the quintessential tourist for long:

> I went to a plot of arable ground where I saw a ploughman
> hold the plough, and myself and one Master Francis Flyer did
> the like one after another, that if we live to be old men we
> may say in our old age, we had once holden the plough in
> the Trojan territories...

It is unclear where Coryat went from Troy, but it wasn't somewhere to stay, by any means. He was in Constantinople on 1 April to visit a group of flagellants in the Franciscan monastery there shortly before midnight. The word 'visit', however, doesn't quite catch the right tone. Coryat had come to see them perform. It was the fashionable thing to do: with him in the audience were many gentlemen of quality and the French ambassador to boot.

Shortly after mass a group of men prostrated themselves before the high altar, 'whipped themselves very cruelly and continued in the merciless punishment of themselves at the least an hour and a half'. At first Coryat assumed that the men must be friars themselves, but he soon discovered his mistake: '[the friars] love to spare their flesh, though it be otherwise reported of them,' he noted. In fact these men were galley slaves who, in order to earn their freedom, undertook these punishments on behalf of 'the richer sort' in lieu of the latter's penance for any sins confessed at Easter. 'The poor villains did endure such bitter chastisement which they inflicted upon themselves that I could scarce behold them with dry eyes,' Coryat wrote. 'Their faces were covered with canvas veils so that no man could perceive them, and all the middle part of their back was naked.' On the end of each lash was a sharp piece of iron, which 'at the first blow it laid upon the skin did easily draw blood'. One of the men, he noted, was 'a little faster than the rest, [and had] flayed all the skin from his back; a very doleful and tragic spectacle'. Most, however, 'favoured themselves more than this man did'. All the while the friars hovered, ministering to the men's wounds with vinegar-soaked cloths, wiping away the blood, keeping them clean. As entertainment Coryat found it all 'terrible and cruel'.

Constantinople itself held him until the end of the year. He was lucky, as he often was, in his company: here he was staying with the English Ambassador, Sir Paul Pinder, who supplied his every want. Not everything he did was as unpredictable or unpleasant as the flagellants. On 28 April he rose at five in the morning to see the Grand Seignior enter the city from Adrianople: 'The pomp of it was so gallant that I never saw the like in my life; neither do I think that the like hath been used among any princes of the world, save these Musulmen, since the times of the triumphs of the Roman Emperors.' Coryat reckoned that the retinue numbered 15,000. Other spectacles drew him also: fireworks lit on 16 boats across the Bosphorus, with great castles and cypress trees hanging amid the smoke in the dark sky; the Vizier's three sons parading on horseback with jewels hanging from their turbans, black ostrich feathers and vests of gold cloth, the saddles they sat made of silver plate.

Coryat remained in Constantinople through the heat of the summer, when the sun scorched all the grass and grasshoppers, brought in on the east wind, fell so thickly that they seemed to blanket the rooftops and people couldn't walk the streets without treading on them. The evening brought forth the fireflies, which drifted in the air like embers. Coryat discovered, too, if he didn't already know, that customs were very different outside Christendom:

The Turk doth never at the saluting of his friend at any time
of the day, or when drinking to him at dinner or supper, put
off his turban, but boweth his head and putteth his right

hand upon his breast; so that he utterly disliketh the fashion
that is used among us of putting off our hats. Therefore when
he wisheth any ill to his enemy he prayeth God to send him
no more rest than to a Christian's hat.

Coryat left Constantinople for Jerusalem, aboard an English ship,
the *Great Defence*, on 21 January 1613. There was snow for two days
and nights, and contrary winds, and there was a thick mist about
Gallipoli for three days more. In Aleppo he was again befriended
by the English consul, another Somerset man named Bartholomew
Haggat, who hooked him up with a caravan, which left on 13 March.
Aleppo seemed a town surrounded by water, but it was only fields
of wild thyme with its white sprigs of flowers rolling in the breeze.
Ten days later the caravan had made it to Damascus, where 'all
things conspired to an earthly paradise'. Coryat saw a mosque with
as many pillars as there are days of the year and five brazen gates, 40
feet high. He had heard that, so beautiful was the city, the Grand
Seignior could not live there lest he should forfeit his hopes of
paradise.

By 12 April Coryat had made it to Jerusalem, where the Turks
made all the Christian members of the caravan pay to redeem their
heads at the gates of the city. Once inside, the Franciscan friars took
the travellers up to their monastery and washed their feet. On Palm
Sunday, for reasons that are unexplained, Coryat slept in the upper
gallery of a temple and was roused by Greeks coming out of their
choir shouting,

> with eleven banners of silk and cloth of gold carried before
> them, each of which had three streamers, and on the top of
> the staff a golden cross. A world of lamps was carried before
> and behind them, men women, children confusedly crying
> Kyrie Eleison.

Visiting the Mount of Olives, he saw a rock which bore the impression of two feet, such as would be made in soft earth by a man getting
ready to leap.

It was in Jerusalem, too, that Coryat had a tattoo[9] of the cross placed on each of his wrists. He was very proud of them, since they were 'as if they had been drawn by some accurate pencil upon parchment'. Later Coryat would show them to people and quote from the Bible: 'I bear in my body the marks of the Lord Jesus.'

Outside the city, between Jerusalem and Bethlehem, Coryat visited a rock on which, it was said, Mary had sat down to feed the baby Jesus, and which had yielded to her body like a cushion. At the River Jordan, to great applause, he saw men, women and children strip naked in the hope that the river would wash away their sins. It was, though, he observed, very muddy; some were up to their middle in mud as they stood close to the banks. Not far from there, Coryat heard, was the pillar of Lot's wife, who was turned to salt. There was a child in her arms and, nearby, a pet dog in salt, too, however unbiblical that might be. His interpreter said that 50 years earlier his father had seen a finger broken off, which had then regrown.

Coryat stayed about a month in Jerusalem before returning to Aleppo, where he remained for three months before taking a caravan into Persia, past the Euphrates, 'the chiefest of all that irrigated paradise'. Four days from Aleppo he and his companions came to Mesopotamia. Another two days brought them to Ur, where Abraham was born, a very delicate and pleasant city, Coryat thought, in which he totally failed to find the ruins of Abraham's house, despite spending four days looking. From there it was another four days to the Tigris, again with some disappointment, for it was 'so shallow that it reached no higher than the calf of my leg [when] I waded over it afoot'.

All in all, it took a little over four months to reach Lahore, 'one of the largest cities of the whole universe', from Aleppo. From Lahore it took another 20 days to reach Agra, along a straight, shady, tree-lined road called the Long Walk. Finally, there was a ten-day trek to the court of the 'Moguls' (Mughals is the contemporary term) at

9. Actually, we don't know what the name of the process was, but from the description that is clearly what it is. The word 'tattoo' entered the English language only after James Cook's expedition to Tahiti in 1769.

Ajmer. Throughout the entire journey from Aleppo, Coryat reckoned, he had spent no more than £3, yet he had 'fared reasonable well every day; victuals being so cheap in some countries where I travelled that oftentimes I lived comfortably for a penny a day'. Of those 60 shillings he was cheated out of ten by some Armenian Christians. Drinking, he added, cost nothing, since he rarely drank anything other than water.

In Ajmer he was the guest of the newly established East India Company, which had established its first 'factory' (that is, trading post) at Surat in 1612. He stayed with them for a year, avoiding paying for food or lodging or laundry. He also made friends with Sir Thomas Roe[10], the English Ambassador to the court of the Great Mogul – Ben Jonson was a mutual friend – and Roe's chaplain, Edward Terry. It is Terry who has left us another character sketch of Coryat, which, while still friendly, is a good deal sourer than that of Jonson, who, let's be honest, was not usually shy about highlighting the faults of his friends. Terry says that Coryat had

> great knowledge of language but [was] not a little ignorant of
> himself, he being so covetous for praise that he would hear
> and endure more of it that he could in any measure deserve;
> being like a ship that hath too much sail and too little
> ballast.

The only reason he had undertaken his travels was 'the hope of that glory which he should reap after he had finished his long travels [which] made him not at all to take notice of the hardship he found in them'. He was therefore devastated to hear it reported that King James I, on hearing Coryat's name in conversation, had asked: 'Is that fool yet living?'

In Ajmer Coryat reported that, each year, the Mogul had himself weighed on a set of golden scales and gave away to the poor the gold weights that counterbalanced him. In his menagerie there were two

10. Thanks to the eccentric captain Luke Foxe, Roe is remembered on maps in a part of the world that he never actually visited: see the Survivor's Tale.

unicorns, as well as lions, elephants, leopards, bears and antelopes.[11] Twice a week the elephants fought in front of the Mogul, being made to 'justle together like two little mountains' and, eventually, parted by fireworks. Coryat claimed, somewhat implausibly, that the menagerie cost £10,000 a day to run.

Before he left Ajmer Coryat had learned enough Hindustani – adding it to his Persian, Turkish, Arabic and Italian – to make an oration before the Mogul, though he had to do so behind Roe's back, since the ambassador did not want an Englishman to be seen importuning money, which he had a shrewd idea Coryat would do. In the event, Coryat described himself as 'a poor traveller and world-seer which am come from a far country, namely England, which ancient historians thought to have been sit in the farthest bounds of the West, and which is the queen of all the islands in the world'. Then, rather strangely, he expressed a 'desire to see the blessed sepulchre of the lord of the corners' – better known as Tamerlane – adding that 'perhaps he is not altogether so famous in his own country of Tartaria as in England'. This is doubly strange, since, aside from Marlowe's play, *Tamburlaine the Great*, Tamerlane wasn't at all famous in England either. The Mogul explained he had no sway over that region and that any pass he might offer to Coryat would effectively be his death warrant if he tried to use it. Nevertheless, before the Mogul disappeared from the window at which he had been holding audience, he threw down a sheet, tied by the four corners, with a hundred pieces of silver wrapped within it.

Coryat left Ajmer on 12 September 1616. His last known piece of correspondence was a letter to his mother dated 31 October. The last time Terry and Roe saw him they were standing together in a room, Coryat against a stone pillar, when Coryat fainted. He begged them, 'if he should die on his way to Surat, that he might not be buried in obscurity, and none of his friends ever knew what became of him'.

Perhaps he had a presentiment, perhaps he was simply feeling old and ill, but in Surat, on meeting the English factors there, he demanded some drink of them – according to Terry's later account,

11. When this was published in *Purchas's Pilgrimages* (1625).

'crying "Sack, sack, is there such a thing as sack? I pray give me some sack."' However much he drank, it was too much and his constitution, which otherwise must have been elephantine, gave way at last.

He was buried, some time in December 1616, says Terry, a little outside the town of Swally, by the sea, 'under a little monument like one in an English churchyard'. His no doubt voluminous notes, collected over the previous 10 years, have never been seen and his grave is long gone. It is a nice irony that a domed Islamic tomb on the shore there has somehow come to be marked on Admiralty maps as 'Tom Coryat's tomb'.

The Mapmakers' Tales

We review the ridiculous errors of cartographers in the South Pacific and consider the strange, intermittent existence of the remotest island on the planet

*T*he early mapmakers are, of course, a source of much trouble. They habitually turned rumours and stories into definitive truths, and, in so doing, displayed an unfortunate combination of naiveté and conservatism. Always keen to be the first to display new findings about the shape of the world, they were no less reluctant to remove past mistakes. It is, after all, hard to disprove the existence of things – even things as large as islands – just because they have temporarily been mislaid.

Not content to rely on the gossip they picked up on quaysides, or scraps of third-hand information allegedly culled from ancient texts, the mapmakers had no ethical problems when it came to inking in areas on their maps that they thought ought to exist. While our understanding of mapmaking would usually be confined to the careful marking of the known, medieval and Renaissance cartographers had a rather more generous conception of their role. They were philosophical geographers. Worse, perhaps, they were *theoretical* philosophical geographers. They liked to extrapolate, on the basis of fashionable theory, what might be out there, still undiscovered. While some were happy to let unknown coasts stay unmarked – the unbroken lines of peninsulas, points and coves tailing off, like loose threads or trains of thought, in open space – others had no apparent qualms about setting down their ideas and sending them out into the world, as if to say, 'This is so.'

There's no better example of this caste of mind than Terra Australis Incognita, the 'unknown southern land', roughly (often very roughly) corresponding to what we know as Antarctica. The key word here is *incognita*, 'unknown'. No human being is known to have seen Antarctica before about 1820, yet plenty of people had thought that a continent ought to be there and it had been appearing on maps, in wildly different shapes and sizes, since at least 1513. The prevailing theory was that the land masses of the northern hemisphere would be balanced by land masses of more or less equal size in the southern hemisphere. Since almost all of the known world was in the north – all of Europe, Asia and North America, most of Africa and a good chunk of South America – it followed that Terra Australis would be enormous.

So indeed it was, on paper. The great cartographers of the era, including Orontius Fineus, Gerard Mercator – who famously devised the Mercator projection, still in use today – and Abraham Ortelius all showed the southern continent spreading itself gamely over most of the hemisphere. On at least one map it joins South America; on another, a peninsula reaches up towards Java; on all of them it stretches up far inside the temperate zones, far beyond the frozen south.

If this weren't bad enough, the mapmakers covered their tracks thoroughly: the detailed coastlines provided are at once products of pure fantasy and wholly credible. Who could have called their bluff?

When Ortelius, in his *Theatrum Orbis Terrarum* (1571), adorned Tierra del Fuego with an Archipelago de las Islas, or ushered into existence an island called Java Minor, there was next to no one alive who could have gainsaid him. When Mercator identified a portion of Terra Australis as the Land of Parrots, or allocated to it – apparently randomly – some Asian place names drawn from Marco Polo, there were not even many around to point out the absurdity. No one had yet been there.

It was the search for Terra Australis[1] that brought the world the discovery of Bouvet's Island, unarguably the most remote and inhospitable island on the face of the planet. Roughly 90 per cent of its surface is glacier. It is 1,000 miles from anywhere – and, given that the anywhere in question is Antarctica, that's hardly anything to get excited about. The next nearest place is Cape Town, a mere 1,300 miles away. Yet for a small, insignificant speck in the South Atlantic it has been the cause of a surprising degree of contention.

It was first sighted by a French seaman called Jean-Baptiste-Charles de Lozier Bouvet, in command of the *Marie* and the *Aigle*, on 1 January 1739. In foul weather – entirely characteristic for the region – Bouvet saw before him a great headland to the south, which he thought was likely to be the coast of the promised new continent. Of course, if he had bothered to circumnavigate the island, he would have found out for sure, but he didn't. As he was a good Catholic, and 1 January was traditionally understood to be the day on which Christ was circumcised, Bouvet named his discovery Circumcision Island.

---

1. We can't let Terra Australis go by without also mentioning Austrialia del Espíritu Santo, the great continent in the Pacific Ocean, discovered by the Portuguese Pedro Fernando de Quierós on behalf of Spain in 1603. Whatever his other qualities, Quierós certainly had chutzpah. He told Philip III of Spain that he had laid the cornerstone of a city, which he called New Jerusalem, and established a new chivalric order, called the Knights of the Holy Ghost.

More alarmingly, he also claimed that his Austrialia was bigger than Europe and richer than Peru. It was, in fact, one of the islands of Vanuatu, previously known as the New Hebrides, and it wasn't even the biggest one of those. (Although the one he discovered does still bear the name Espiritu Santo.)

Philip declined to finance any further expeditions.

(The name quickly fell from use, although it is still remembered on the island itself in Circumcision Cape towards the northwest.)

Bouvet stayed in the area for ten days, but it proved impossible to land. Eventually, he moved on and returned home. For 30-odd years his discovery was accepted without further trial. Then, in 1772, Captain Cook came searching for it on HMS *Resolution*. He came again in 1775. The following year a Captain Furneaux of the Royal Navy, aboard HMS *Adventure*, did the same. Following the failure on all three occasions to locate anything, Bouvet's Island was discounted: Bouvet must have seen an iceberg, said Cook, dismissively.

The island was eventually rediscovered on 6 October 1808, by James Lindsay, captain of the Enderby brothers' whaler the *Swan*. However, with the island beset with field ice, Lindsay too was unable to land. It is at this point that the story gets complicated, because, when Lindsay reported his finding, no one believed that it was Bouvet's Island, and Lindsay's Island began to appear on maps instead.

Bouvet next appears in the record in 1824, on 6 December to be precise, when an American seaman called Benjamin Morrell arrived in search of seal pelts. He wrote later:

Here... on the western shore, was a fine anchorage, inside of the immense number of ice-islands which lay in that quarter, from one to three miles offshore, all of them aground in from ten to one hundred fathoms of water. Some of these ice-islands were a mile in circumference, and lay so close to each other that it was with difficulty that we got the vessel between them to the anchorage... We finally succeeded, however, and anchored on the northwest side of the island, in seventeen fathoms of water, about half a mile from the shore. In this situation, we lay entirely sheltered, by the ice-islands on one side, and Bouvet's on the other, from whatever point of the compass the wind might blow.

It is from Morrell that we have our first description of the island:

The island is evidently of volcanic origin; even the rocks have been melted by the former eruptions into a complete mass of lava, presenting the appearance of blue and green glass. There are some small spots of vegetation on the hillsides; but the mountain, which rises about three thousand feet above the level of the sea, is covered with pumice-stone... Who can declare how many ages have elapsed since the fires were extinguished which once raged in the bosom of this mountain! — He alone who laid the foundations of the Earth... I have no doubt that there is land in the vicinity of this; and I think the most likely place to seek for it would be to the south.

All well and good. The problem is, though, that Morrell is unreliable. One contemporary described him as 'the biggest liar in the Pacific' and it is too much to hope that circumstances might have been different now that he was in the South Atlantic. Certainly, no one seems to think that he really got to Bouvet's Island. True, his description is broadly accurate; but then, one wonders about that pumice stone; and where are the glaciers?

The very next year, however, on 10 December, Bouvet's Island was rediscovered – again – by the English Captain Norris, commanding the *Sprightly* and the *Lively*. Six days later, he and others from the two ships landed, and claimed the island for Britain. Two days later, two boatloads of crew, sent ashore sealing, were trapped on the island by the weather; it was almost a week before they were relieved. Unfortunately, Norris, believing that Bouvet's Island officially didn't exist, now named the island Liverpool Island. For good measure, he discovered another island nearby, which he called Thompson Island.

There were now four islands, a veritable archipelago, officially occupying roughly the same spot: Bouvet, Liverpool, Lindsay and Thompson. Victorian maps usually showed some of them and at least one shows all four. It wasn't until 1918 that anyone took the next step and concluded that the four were, in point of fact, the same island.

At which moment, you might expect that Bouvet's Island would cease to be of any interest. Not so. In December 1927, it was annexed, somewhat unexpectedly, by Norway.

When it discovered what Norway had done, Britain – which was probably barely aware of the existence of Bouvet's Island, let alone its ownership of the place – feeling that it really ought not to stand for such behaviour, complained to the League of Nations. It would be misleading, however, to say that it complained either loud or long. In 1928, more important things were on the horizon. (Actually, there has never been a year in which more important things than the fate of Bouvet's Island have not been on the horizon.)

Quite what Norway – not, I think it's fair to say, one of the world's greater imperial powers – hoped to gain by the acquisition of an inaccessible and uninhabitable hunk of volcanic rock, mostly covered in ice, at almost exactly the opposite ends of the Earth, is another matter. A couple of huts with provisions for shipwrecked sailors were built – not that there had been any, since the island isn't exactly in the middle of a busy shipping lane. More recently, an unstaffed meteorological station has been added, but other imperial or colonial activity has hitherto been conspicuous by its absence.

The Friar's Tale

Friar Odoric relates his encounters with the Great Khan and various Mongol nobles

Born in around 1286 at Pordenone in northeastern Italy, Friar Odoric was sent by his Franciscan order to Asia some time after 1316. He spent 13 years travelling around the East, including three years in China at the court of the Great Khan, before returning to Italy. Shortly before he died a fellow friar noted down Odoric's account of his journeys. It was well known throughout the 14th century and whoever was actually responsible for the *Travels of Sir John Mandeville* almost certainly had a copy before him as he wrote.

Most medieval travellers go out of their way to deflect accusations of credulity by assuring their readers that they have written only about things of which they have had first-hand experience. Not so Odoric: 'For things such as I saw not myself,' he declares, 'the common talk of those countries beareth witness to their truth.' Given that the things he claimed to have seen himself include two-headed geese in Ceylon, hens that bore wool instead of feathers and an island, called Moumoran, inhabited by dog-headed people,[1] one can have no great hopes for the accuracy of his accounts of things that came to him at second or third hand – and, indeed, we are not disappointed. Thus he says, leaping off at a tangent from a description of one of the Khan's feasts:

> I was informed by certain credible persons that in the mountains of Kapsei, in the kingdom of Kalor, which is in the dominions of the Great Khan, some gourds or pumpkins grow that open when ripe to reveal inside them a little beast that resembles a young lamb. I have heard, too, that certain trees grow on the shores of the Irish Sea, which bear a gourd-like fruit that fall into the sea at particular times of the year, and are changed into birds called barnacles. And this is most true.

However, without wishing to state the obvious, the difference between Mandeville and Odoric is that Mandeville himself is almost certainly a fiction, whereas Odoric at least has the advantage of having actually lived and breathed. At least, one assumes that he did, since he was later beatified by the Catholic Church. It is hard to know, therefore, what we should make of experiences such as this, which probably befell him – the details are somewhat vague – somewhere in southern China or, as he knew it, Mancy:

> Another great and terrible thing I saw. For, as I went through a certain valley by the river of delights, I saw many corpses

---

1. It's strange to note that Odoric was an almost exact contemporary of his fellow Franciscan William of Ockham, deviser of Ockham's razor, a principle that states that, where competing explanations for phenomena are available, one should always choose the simplest. One wonders what they would have talked about if they had ever met.

lying. And I heard also sundry kinds of music, but chiefly
nakers [kettle drums], which were marvellously played upon.
And so great was the noise that very great fear came upon
me. Now this valley is seven or eight miles long and if any
unbeliever enters, he will never quit it, but will perish. Yet I
hesitated not to enter, that I might see what the matter was.
And when I had gone in I saw, as I have said, such number of
corpses as no one without seeing it could deem credible. And
at one side of the valley, in the very rock, I saw the face of a
man very great and very terrible, so very terrible indeed that
for my exceeding great fear my spirit seemed to die in me.
Wherefore I made the sign of the cross, and began
continually to repeat *Verbum caro factum* – the word became
flesh – but I dared not at all to approach that face, but kept
at seven or eight paces from it. And so I came at length to
the other side of the valley, climbed a hill of sand and looked
around me. I could see nothing, but the drums continued to
sound. At the very top of the hill I found a great quantity of
silver heaped up as if it had been fishes' scales, and some of
this I put into my bosom. But as I cared nought for it, and
was at the same time in fear lest it should be a snare to
hinder my escape, I cast it all down again to the ground. And
so by God's grace I came forth scatheless.

Terror, riches, sensory overload, death: it could be the template for
all medieval travels in the East. Indeed, Odoric's travels are in many
ways a hymn to the terrible majesty and wealth of the court of the
Great Khan at Cambaleth[2] – Khanbaliq, or modern Beijing, the capital of the Mongol empire since Kublai Khan had made it so in 1267:

Being taken by the Tartars,[3] they built a new city at the
distance of half a mile, which they named Caido, which has
twelve gates, each two miles distant from the other. The

2. Or Cambalu or Cambalec: take your pick. See also the Merchant's Tale.
3. It was customary in medieval Europe to conflate Tartars (or Tatars) with Mongols

space also between the two cities is thoroughly built upon, and inhabited; so that the whole is as one city, and is forty miles in circuit. In this city the Great Khan or Emperor has his palace, the walls of which are four miles in circuit; and near to the imperial palace there are many other houses and palaces of the nobles who belong to the court. Within the precincts of the imperial palace, there is a most beautiful mount, all set over with trees, called the Green Mount, having a sumptuous palace on the top, in which the Khan mostly resides. On one side of the mount is a great lake, abounding in geese and ducks, and all manner of water fowl, and having a most magnificent bridge; and the wood upon the mount is stored with all kinds of beasts and land birds. Hence when the Khan is inclined to take the diversion of hunting or hawking, he needs not to quit his palace.

When the Khan sat on the imperial throne, his chief consort was on his left, and his eldest son and heir on his right. Below them sat the other members of the imperial family. All the married ladies wore headdresses shaped like a man's foot but about 30 inches long; each was decorated with cranes' feathers and extravagantly set with pearls. Standing to attention, but in perfect silence, were the noblemen and their retinues, together with four secretaries tasked with taking down every word that the Great Khan spoke.

On feast days the Khan was attended by some 14,000 'barons' (as Odoric identifies the leading Mongol courtiers), their heads crowned with gold coronets, their bodies dressed in cloth of gold studded with precious stones. Each outfit, says Odoric, was worth 10,000 florins. Everyone, from the noblemen down, knew their place; and everyone, despite the vast numbers of staff, had a place, too. There were at least 18 *tomans* of stage-players, musicians, and such like – a toman being a military unit 10,000 strong – and 15 of the keepers of dogs, other beasts and fowl.[4] The Khan himself had 400 physicians, eight of whom were Christians and one a Saracen.

4. Odoric's estimate, therefore, of 330,000.

There were four great feasts each year, celebrating the Khan's birth, his circumcision, his enthronement and his marriage. The colours were gorgeous (Coryat wouldn't have approved): the highest nobility were dressed in green, the members of the next rank in red and the lowest-ranking in yellow. All wore golden girdles 'half a foot broad' and held ivory tablets in their hand, standing still and reverently silent. 'In one of the corners of a certain great gallery, all the philosophers or magicians attend, waiting for certain hours and moments, and when the fortunate moment is arrived, a crier calleth out in a loud voice, "Prostrate yourselves before the Emperor," and then all fall upon their faces'. This was standard stuff, to an extent, although the following injunction from the philosophers, 'for every one to stop their ears with their fingers', and many similar things, seem, even to Odoric, to be 'vain and ridiculous'. These exercises were followed by musicians and women singers, whom he found delightful, and:

> After them, the lions are led in, and are made to pay their
> obeisance to the Emperor. Then the jugglers cause golden
> cups, full of wine, to fly up and down in the air, and to apply
> themselves to men's mouths, that they may drink. And many
> other strange things are performed, which I omit to mention,
> as no one would believe me.

On this last point, at least, Odoric was certainly right. The scale of what he describes undoubtedly seems exaggerated, if not entirely fanciful. Strangely, more memorable in a way is Odoric's description of a brief chance encounter with the Great Khan himself. Perhaps it lodged in Odoric's memory, too, since it is the very last image in his narrative.

A day or two's journey out of Cambalec, Odoric was walking with four others of his order, one of whom was a bishop. The sun was high and, growing hot, they stopped to rest beneath a broad tree. Soon they became aware that Khan was approaching with his retinue. The friars leapt up, lest they be thought disrespectful, and began to sing *Veni, Creator Spiritus* – 'Come, Holy Spirit' – while the bishop pulled on his vestments and raised aloft a cross strapped to the end of his staff. Hearing them sing, the Khan, who lay out of sight within his palanquin, ordered his vast entourage to stop. Then he summoned the Franciscans to him. They approached the still, silent mass of courtiers, servant and soldiers, chanting as they went, and the bishop presented the cross for the Khan to kiss. With his followers looking on, the Khan slowly raised himself and, leaning forward, did as he was bid, bringing his face but a few feet from the Franciscans below. Usually no one was suffered to come within a stone's throw of the Khan's palanquin, so this was, in its own way, an extraordinary act, a benediction of his own to Odoric and the others. The bishop blessed him and, since it was customary for those who met the Khan to bring him gifts, Odoric offered all they had: a small dish of apples. The Khan, ruler of the greatest empire in the world, considered the gift and silently took two. One he bit into crisply; the other he held thoughtfully in his hand. He and his attendants then turned away, and passed slowly out of sight along the hot dusty road.

It had been Kublai Khan who had, in 1267, moved the capital of the vast Mongol realm to Cambaleth. Previously the capital had been the city established by his grandfather, Genghis Khan: Karakorum, on the banks of the Orhun River in northern Mongolia. It was from there that Genghis had launched his conquest of China in 1211. Karakorum's heyday as a capital was brief, then, and its decline was swift: it was destroyed by the Chinese in 1388 and rediscovered only in 1898. (The whole Orkhon Valley, in which the ruins stand, is now a World Heritage Site.)

Looking at contemporary descriptions, however, one can see why Genghis and his successors might have thought the grass was greener elsewhere – because it was. The first western visitor to the court at Karakorum was Giovanni Da Pian Del Carpini, a Franciscan friar, who, at 60, was already an old man by medieval standards,[5] and in this instance an ambassador for Pope Innocent IV. He arrived at Karakorum on 22 July 1246. He was not impressed – at least, not by the country itself, for he was never actually allowed into the city.

5. He had in fact been a disciple of St Francis himself.

It was, in his estimation, sandy and barren, whether on the plains or the mountains, with precious little water anywhere. Consequently, not one part in a hundred, he said, was fruitful and the land was good for nothing but raising cattle. There were so few trees, in fact, that in place of fire wood, the Tartars used cattle dung.

He was even less impressed with the climate. Winter, he noted, was wholly without rain. Summer, on the other hand, brought deadly thunderstorms and either extreme heat or extreme cold. The storms were sometimes accompanied by blizzards – and such strong, bitter winds that you couldn't even stay on your horse. On one occasion, he recalled, the winds were so fierce that everyone lay grovelling on the ground, blinded by the dirt. At the Emperor's coronation, similarly, so much hail fell that, when it melted, some 160 people drowned.

Can we take such claims seriously? Carpini, after all, is by no means the least reliable and observant of European travellers – and he claims to have attended this very coronation. How much hail, though, would it take to drown 160 people? The fact is that the very mention of the Great Khan or Karakorum brought out the very worst hyperbole in westerners. On one level it was simply that they found the scale of the Mongol empire and its wealth impossible to communicate. On another, it was that they themselves could not process all the information their senses were being bombarded with – not just the riches and the rituals, the variety and expanse. It was the strangeness and difference of it – the sheer alien unknown – too.

The Drunkard's Tale

We discover how little common sense the English government had when it came to promises of gold in the New World – and also how poor was the geography of one of our greatest poets

Hearsay is a strange and powerful thing. For centuries it was the cornerstone of cartographical research, unreliable but utterly indispensable. Herodotus's *Histories* are a monument to it. Yet few stories demonstrate the ability of hearsay to get things horribly wrong better than that of the kingdom of Norumbega, at the head of the Penobscot River in Maine.

The trouble, as was often the case, began with a map. Specifically, it was the map drawn up by Girolamo de Verrazzano to record his brother Giovanni's voyage up the eastern seaboard of North

America in 1524. On an otherwise unremarkable stretch of New England coastline, Girolamo wrote the single word – perhaps a name – '*oranbega*'. No one actually knows what the word refers to or where it comes from. Some argue that it was a local Native American word meaning 'a stretch of placid water between rapids'. Others, picking up on its later morphing into 'Norumbega', claim that it is proof of the Viking discovery of North America. (It's a corruption of Norvege, obviously.)

At the time, however, the mysterious word seems to have been taken to mean only one thing: an unknown kingdom. So it was that by 1545, Pierre Crignon could write that:

> Beyond Cape Breton is a land contiguous to that cape, the coast of which travels south-southwestward toward the land called Florida, and for a good 500 leagues... The inhabitants of this country are docile, friendly and peaceful...[1] The land overflows with every kind of fruit; there grow the wholesome orange and the almond, and many sorts of sweet-smelling trees.

Around the same time Jean Alfonce, a French pilot and navigator, was claiming for himself the discovery of the Cap de Norombègue south of Newfoundland, together with a great river.

> Fifteen leagues along this river is a city called Norombègue with clever inhabitants and a mass of peltries of all kind of beasts. The citizens dress in furs, wearing sable cloaks... The people use many words which sound like Latin and worship the sun, and they are fair people and tall.[2]

1. Actually, this was the opposite of Verrazzano's experience. Although he found most of the natives friendly, those along the Maine coast threw things at his men and were fond of standing on the shore, facing inland, bending over and baring their arses in the direction of the white men. Verrazzano called the whole coast Terra Onde di Mala Gente, the 'Land of Bad People'.
2. Although this was published in Alfonce's *Cosmographie* (1559), it's not entirely clear when it was written. Alfonce himself died in 1544. He had a reputation as a brilliant navigator and pilot, but is considered somewhat untrustworthy as a narrator.

All the interest thus far seems to have been French. Soon, however, one David Ingram launched himself on the scene. Ingram was an English seaman from Barking in Essex. He had sailed with Hawkins on an early slaving expedition in 1568. They had run into severe trouble with the Spanish in Mexico and – 'being forced with hunger', in Hawkins's phrase – and fearing that their ships wouldn't make it home, 114 men chose to take their chances on the American mainland. Hawkins put them ashore in the Gulf of Mexico. Most headed west, ultimately to brutal enslavement and death at the hands of the Spanish; three were burned alive. A few, Ingram among them, went north.

It must have seemed a hopeless kind of journey. What, if anything, they had realistic hopes for, beyond mere survival, it's hard to see. Yet slowly they made their way up the eastern seaboard, every few miles one of them scaling a tree or climbing a hill – any kind of vantage point would do – to scout out the land ahead for settlements and other signs of humanity, as well as for natural lifelines such as rivers. Their encounters with the indigenous peoples were tense – the first group they met stripped Ingram and his companions of their clothes in order to marvel at the strange whiteness of their skin – but peaceful. Incredibly, over the course of some eight months, three of Hawkins's men – Ingram himself, Richard Browne and Richard Twite – managed to walk all the way to what is now Maine, in the northeastern United States. There they made contact with a French ship, which – once its men had recovered from the shock of seeing three Englishmen appear from nowhere out of the wilderness of the New World – took them back to Le Havre and thence to England.

Ingram seems to have spent the next 12 years living off his exploits in the inns and taverns of home. He can hardly be blamed if the tale grew a smidgeon in the telling. We would not have heard of him, however, if his exploits had not come to the attention of Elizabeth I's government. Ingram, now aged 40, was summoned for a series of interviews in August and September 1582 before, among others, Elizabeth's Secretary of State, the formidable Sir Francis Walsingham. If Ingram was nervous, he had every cause to be so:

Walsingham, the Queen's spymaster, was not a man either to mislead – or to disappoint.[3]

Whatever else Ingram did, he didn't disappoint. There is no narrative to relate, just a dream-like torrent of images and memories. Norumbega was half a mile long, with many streets far broader than those in London. The kings of the region wore rubies that were six inches long and two inches broad. There was a great abundance of pearls; they could be found in every cottage, 'sometimes a quart, sometimes a pottle, sometimes a peck' (that is, between two pints and two gallons); some were the size of an acorn. If anyone held both his hands out together and kissed the backs of them, it was the greatest token of friendship.

It goes on. Their houses were round like a dovehouse, the roofs supported by pillars of silver, gold and crystal. In each, the meanest domestic items, the scoops, the buckets et al, were made of solid silver. Outside, you could pick up crystals and lumps of gold as big as a man's fist from the river heads. There were sheep which bore red wool; there were elephants; there was 'a kind of fowl, about the same size and shape as a goose [which] haunts the rivers, near unto the islands. The wings are covered with small yellow feathers and cannot fly. You may drive them before you like sheep. They are exceeding fat and very delicate meat. They have white heads, and therefore the countrymen call them penguins, which seems to be a Welsh name.'[4]

Several English voyagers went scuttling off across the Atlantic to make contact with, and – so they hoped – conquer this great realm, with predictable results. Norumbega, for instance, was on Sir

3. We don't know whether the interviews were carried out under duress. In one version of his testimony, still extant, the interrogative nature of the meetings is apparent. All Ingram's answers are preceded with the ominous phrase, 'He hath confessed…' Still, perhaps that was just the standard phrase used, trotted out whatever the circumstances.
4. Ingram adds here: 'They have also in use divers other Welsh words. A matter worth the noting…' This is a nod to the tradition that America had been discovered by the Welsh prince Madoc in 1170. It was said that he established a colony either in Florida or Alabama, on the Gulf of Mexico, and well into the 19th century it was thought that the Mandan tribe on the upper reaches of the Missouri were descended from Welsh stock and spoke a Welsh-inflected language.

Humphrey Gilbert's shopping list on his ill-fated voyage of 1583. Gilbert himself was last seen alive on Monday 9 September when, with his ship being battered by the sea, he sat at the stern of his frigate, book in hand, calling out to fellow seamen in another ship, 'We are as near to Heaven by sea as by land' – which, as last words go, is not at all bad.

But there were others on Gilbert's expedition who also had reason to regret the looseness of Ingram's tongue. Before Gilbert and his frigate went down, another ship on the voyage had already come to grief: the *Delight*, under one Richard Clark of Weymouth, had run aground in rain and thick mist, with the sea 'going mightily and high' in the words of an eye-witness, on Thursday 29 August. The back of the ship, he said, was quickly beaten to pieces, and most of the 100-odd crew were lost.

Clark and 16 of his men got away in a small boat, however. This was unbeknownst to Gilbert and the crews of the other ships, who spent two days risking their own lives, beating up and down as close to the wreck as they dared, and scouring the sea for survivors. But the men were drifting. The 17 survivors had just one oar to work their boat, which must have been next to useless. The land was 70 leagues away and the storm made raising sail impossible. Seventeen, however, was too many men for the boat, and one of them, Mr Hedly by name, soon suggested that the men draw lots. Those with the four shortest should be cast overboard – unless one of them happened to be the master. Clark rejected the idea, grimly: they would, he said, live or die together.

Luckily, on the fifth day, Hedly himself died, and then another of the men, which made the boat a little more seaworthy. But nevertheless, things were hardly good: for five days and five nights they saw the sun and stars just once. They had nothing to eat save whatever weeds they could dredge from the sea; and nothing to drink but saltwater.

But, on the seventh day, came redemption. At about 11 o'clock in the morning they saw land, and at about about three o'clock that afternoon they fell gratefully on the shores of Newfoundland. They had the wind to thank: if it hadn't blown southerly for the whole of their time on the water, they would never have seen land again. Now, within half an hour of their reaching safety, it swung round to the north. They knelt down, every one of them, and gave heartfelt thanks to God. No doubt harsher words were reserved for Ingram.

But Ingram, in fact, has the rare distinction of having had his narrative withdrawn from Hakluyt's *Voyages and Discoveries* between the edition of 1589 and that of 1598–1600. Perhaps it was simply the fact that Norumbega was looking suspiciously non-existent by the close of the century, or perhaps Hakluyt, looking again at the testimony, concluded that too much of it was out-and-out nonsense. English ships had penetrated the Penobscot River by this time and had found little more than a log cabin with some 400 pelts for sale. (Which didn't stop them claiming the land for England, just in case.)

The French were coming to the same conclusion. In 1602 Samuel de Champlain sailed up the Penobscot to the site of modern Bangor, Maine:

> [Some] assert that there is a big town inhabited by skilled and clever savages, who use cotton. I am convinced that the greater part of those who mention it never saw it, and speak of it only in hearsay… That anyone ever entered the river is unlikely, or they would have described it differently.

Marc Lescarbot, sailing with Pierre de Guast, Sieur de Monts, in 1604, is yet more acerbic: 'If this beautiful town hath ever been in nature, I would fain know who hath pulled it down. For there is but cabins here and there… covered with barks of trees, or with skins.'

All of which makes John Milton look rather ridiculous, when, more than 60 years later, he is found still referring to the existence of Norumbega in *Paradise Lost*. It appears in the middle of a long passage (Book X, lines 668–700) – but then, all passages in *Paradise Lost* are long passages – in which Milton tries to sit on the fence about whether the sun revolves around the Earth or vice versa.

It's ironic that Milton, the ultimate bookish poet, should get this kind of information so badly wrong. If only he had frequented a few harbours or quaysides, he would probably have found hearsay to be more *au courant* than the latest reprint of Mercator or Ortelius.

However, he certainly doesn't help his credibility by referring to 'cold Estotiland' a few lines earlier. Estotiland was an island in the North Atlantic which the likes of Mercator and Hakluyt believed to have been discovered in 1390 by two Venetian brothers named Zeno. Their adventures are too extensive to go into here, but alongside Estotiland, they also 'discovered' the islands of Frisland, Drogeo and Icaria. (Frobisher, in fact, following Mercator, believed that he landed on and claimed Frisland for Elizabeth I on 20 June 1578. He renamed it West England, giving one headland the rather unromantic name Charing Cross.) In any event, besides not actually existing, there's nothing in the Zeno brothers' narrative to support Milton's claim that Estotiland was cold. On the contrary, it was rich in everything – 'abounding in all the commodities of the world' – including, of course, gold. In an echo of the island of paradise, often at the back of explorers' minds, at its centre is a high mountain from which four rivers flow.

The Cannibal's Tale

*Several seamen make the ultimate sacrifice in
Newfoundland – albeit unwillingly*

*I*n the 1820s Benjamin Morrell could still state confidently that the Maoris of New Zealand ate their enemies. As late as the early 20th century stories were still circulating about cannibals on the borders of Arakan, a strip of land along the west coast of Burma; in the remoter regions of the Chota Nagpur Plateau in central India; and in New Guinea. Perhaps they circulate still. It's a suspicion heard half-whispered behind almost every encounter between 'civilization' and 'savages'. Dionyse Settle, who sailed with Frobisher on his second voyage to Meta Incognita, simply assumed that the natives they encountered were cannibals because they ate their meat raw, 'as they find it and without any other dressing, a loathsome thing either to the beholders or the hearers'.[1]

It is perhaps ironic, then, that the most direct confirmations of cannibalism actually occurring are in the testimonies of the stranded and shipwrecked of the European diaspora – and it was the Europeans doing the eating.

Take, for example, Robert Hore's voyage to Newfoundland out of Gravesend in April 1536, as recalled by Thomas Buts, a survivor, some 50 years later. (Hakluyt was so desperate to hear Buts's story that he rode some 200 miles to record his experiences.) It was an anomalous voyage in some ways, predating the period in which the far side of the Atlantic gripped the English imagination with its possibilities. And its social mix reminds us that it was not uncommon for Tudor gentlemen to join such explorations in search of glory, wealth and adventure.[2] In Hore's case, he talked some 30 gentlemen into accompanying him – drawn from Henry VIII's court, the Inns of Court and Chancery, and elsewhere.

In any event, Hore's two ships, the *Trinity* and the *Minion*, took a total of 120 men across the Atlantic to Cape Breton. It was a long journey – lasting two months – during which, presumably mistakenly, they made no landfall. They were far enough north that, even sailing in the summer months, they watched in awe as icebergs – 'mighty islands of ice' – drifted by, noting, no doubt a little wistfully, how seabirds used them to rest while on their own transatlantic odysseys.

There's no record of what stores they had on board, but after that length of time, little can have been savoury. Certainly, when they hit

1. This sort of advice, from Sebastian Cabot to the crew of a ship bound for Cathay in 1553, cannot have helped: 'There be people that can swim in the sea, havens, and rivers, naked, having bows and shafts, coveting to draw nigh your ships, which if they shall find not well watched, or warded, they will assault, desirous of the bodies of men, which they covet for meat… diligent watch is to be kept both day and night.'
2. The most well known is probably John Donne, another Inns of Court man, who wrote two verse letters, 'The Calm' and 'The Storm', as a result of his experiences on Raleigh's Azores expedition of 1597. But there is also the example of Thomas Lodge, who wrote *Rosalynde*, from which Shakespeare lifted the plot of *As You Like It* – 'hatched in the storms of the ocean,' Lodge said, when 'every line was wet with a surge' – to pass the time while sailing to the Canaries in 1590.

the coasts of the New World they fell with delight upon 'great fowls white and grey, as big as geese', gorging on their eggs and then flaying, dressing and eating the 'very good and nourishing' birds themselves.

They moved further north and then rode at anchor, hoping to get sight of 'the naturall people of the country'. A London merchant, Oliver Dawbeney, was the first to do so, out walking on the hatches one day, his eyes scanning the shoreline. A boat was rowing towards the ships across the bay. Dawbeney called his friends up on board and they chose to row out to meet the natives halfway. The natives responded by turning their boat around and fleeing to an island, melting quickly away amid its pine and fir trees. The Englishmen found no more than a trace of them: a fire and the side of a bear on a wooden spit, abandoned in haste; a leather boot embroidered – 'garnished with certain brave trails' – with something akin to silk; and 'a great warm mitten'. These early souvenirs they carried gingerly back to the ship.

Wildlife was scarce and they could find nothing now to eat. They took to making trips onto the mainland, greedily grabbing up what mouthfuls of herbs and roots they could.[3] It was at this point, with no end to their famine in sight, that one shipmate first murdered another as he stooped to snatch a meagre root from the ground. The murderer then 'cut out pieces of his body, broiled the same on coals and greedily devoured him'.

It's not clear how long this went on for, although the officers'

---

3. Buts said that the men got some small respite from drinking fresh spring water out of wooden cups in which they had previously drunk a cordial called *aqua composita*, recommended as a palliative for consumption, but also drunk for pleasure. The recipe for *aqua composita* is as follows. Take:

— one gallon of Gascony wine;
— one dram each of ginger, galingale [a kind of mild ginger], cinnamon, and nutmegs;
— one dram each of anis seeds, fennel seeds and caraway seeds; and
— one handful each of sage, mint, red roses, thyme, pellitory [also known as Spanish camomile and effective against toothache], rosemary, wild thyme, camomile and lavender.

Pound the spices and bruise the herbs. Let it all steep for 12 hours and then distil. The recipe is good for one pint for every gallon of wine.

incomprehension at the mysteriously dwindling numbers of crew is almost comic. Before too long, another man out on the mainland scented cooked meat across the air. He grabbed the wrong end of the stick and berated the murderer for letting his comrades starve while he gorged himself. Tempers flared and the latter eventually spat back the immortal words: 'If thou wouldst needs know, the broiled meate that I had was a piece of such a man's buttock.'

Oddly, there is no mention of punishment for the cannibal. Hore gathered the men together and reminded them how abhorrent such things were in the sight of God. If it pleased God not to help them, he said, then it would be better to die.

However, as time went on and their hunger failed to abate, Hore and his crew changed their minds. They had got as far as casting lots to see who should be killed when a well-stocked French ship rode into the harbour. That night the Englishmen overpowered the French and stole away with their ship, making landfall at St Ives in Cornwall towards the end of October 1536. Such was the mercy of God, they said. The French can hardly have taken the same view; when they made it home, they formally complained to Henry VIII, who, 'so moved with pity' for the plight of his subjects, 'punished [them] not, but of his owne purse made full and royal recompense unto the French'.

Buts told Hakluyt that he himself 'was so changed in the voyage with hunger and miserie' that his father and mother didn't recognize him, and indeed refused to acknowledge him until they found a birthmark on one of his knees.

The
Apprentice's
Tale

*The commercial basis of the early British Empire is
revealed to be somewhat lacking*

L ooking back, attempting to short-circuit the centuries of
hindsight that crowd our perspective, what may strike us
most about the European discoveries is the innocence of
it all. That's not to excuse the bloodshed or the rapacity that ensued
– but to recognise the extent to which the rapid expansion of geographical knowledge to all points of the compass blew open their
imaginations. It is interesting, therefore, to revisit the world as they
must have experienced it: a once narrow place which seemed to have
suddenly fallen open, daily spilling out new prodigies, riches and rev-
elations. Who knew what was true any more? The ancients were in
part a guide, but they obscured more than they enlightened, and the

mere fact of the New World's unheralded existence made the short-comings of classical learning when applied to the contemporary abundantly clear.

Trade became, as well as a motive, a means to an end. It offered a path to world power, not simply through the wealth accrued but through the knowledge accumulated. The ships that went out at the merchants' behest, sniffing out new routes to old markets and new markets for surplus stocks, were more than just commercial enterprises. They were tracers sent over the dark horizon, at once tentative and reckless, hard-nosed and naive, and those who waited behind at the quayside were impatient for more than profit. They were impatient too for any points of light that returning ships could bring from the darkness.[1]

We can see the competing claims with which the seamen had to contend and sense the blankness of the map onto which they ventured in Richard Hakluyt's instructions to two such men, Arthur Pet and Charles Jackman, issued in 1580, as they set out under the aegis of the Muscovy Company to find a 'northeast passage' – that is, over the north of Europe – to the wealth of China. If Hakluyt's advice is anything to go by, the Englishmen knew almost nothing, and Hakluyt himself is wishful in the extreme. His was a world-view in which English interpolation anywhere on the globe was an obvious right and no less obvious a good. It was not that he was oblivious to other peoples and cultures, it was simply that couldn't understand that they might prefer things of their own. Thus he wrote to Jackman and Pet:

> Note all the islands and set them down [on a map] to two ends: that we may devise to take the benefit by them; and also foresee how by them the savages or civil princes may in any sort annoy us in our purposed trade that way. And for

1. Paradoxically, perhaps, purely commercial voyages, as opposed to quasi-military ones such as Raleigh's, were highly risk-averse. Pet and Jackman, whom we are shortly to meet, were instructed by Hakluyt 'Not to venture the loss of any one man. You must have great care to preserve your people, since your number is so small, and not to venture any one man in any wise.'

that the people to the which we purpose in this voyage to go be no Christians, it were good that the mass of our commodities were always in our own disposition, and not at the will of others. Therefore it were good that we did seek out some small island in the Scythian sea, where we might plant, fortify, and staple safely, from whence (as time should serve) we might feed those heathen nations with our commodities without cloying them, or without venturing our whole mass in the bowels of their country.

With sublime ignorance of geography, he goes on to fantasise that such an island might lure the Chinese navy to buy their goods there.

Moving on to islands that the English were at least aware of, such as Novaya Zemlya, Hakluyt zealously suggests that 'if you find the soil planted with people, it is like that in time an ample vent of our warm woollen clothes may be found'. This point is underlined by an earnest-seeming marginal note – 'A good consideration' – as if the concept of warm clothing was unlikely to have occurred to anyone already living above the Arctic Circle. Contrariwise, if the islands were unpeopled yet temperate, Hakluyt had another solution: 'We may plant on that main the offals of our people… and so they may in our fishing in our passage, and divers ways yield commodity to England by harbouring and victualling us.' Everything must be noted: high land or low; mountain, or flat; gravelly, clay, chalky; woody or not woody; with springs and rivers or not, and with what wild beasts stocked; whether there is stone to build with, or stone to make lime with, and wood or coal to burn; what kind of timber there might be, whether useful for pitch, tar, masts, dealboard or clapboard, or for building ships or houses; the quality of the havens and harbours; and the existence of straits, and whether they are straight or narrow. All the sailors on the voyage are to swear oaths 'to keep close all such things, that other princes prevent us not of the same'.

The intent is not yet empire, it is wealth. Pet and Jackman are entreated to work out how:

the savage may be made able to purchase our cloth and

[satisfy his] other wants. If you find a populous island, and that the same people hath need of cloth, then are you to devise what commodities they have to purchase the same. If they be poor, then are you to consider of the soil, and how by any possibility the same may be made to enrich them, that hereafter they may have something to purchase the cloth withal.

Indeed, there is almost nothing that Jackman and Pet are not adjured to record or collect. Sometimes this has clear commercial imperatives: they are, for instance, to bring back as many varities of fruits as they can, dried and preserved as necessary. Failing that, seeds, kernels or stones would do since 'such seeds of fruits and herbs coming from another part of the world, and so far off, will delight the fancy of many for the strangeness, and for that the same may grow, and continue the delight long time.'

Sometimes, though, knowledge is required almost for its own sake:

If you arrive at Cambalu or Quinsay, to bring thence the map of that country, for so shall you have the perfect description, which is to great purpose. [Also] bring thence some old printed book, to see whether they have had print there before it was devised in Europe, as some write.

In some respects, it is as if Jackman and Pet were perceived as moving through a tableau, life breathless and still about them, so that they may better reckon its vastness and value, and note all that is required:

If you arrive in Cambalu or Quinsay, to take a special view of their navy, and to note the force, greatness, manner of building of them, the sails, the tackles, the anchors, the furniture of them, with ordinance, armour and munition. Also, to note the force of the walls and bulwarks of their cities, their ordinance, and whether they have any calivers [muskets], and what powder and shot. To note what armour they have. What swords. What pikes, halberds and bills. What horses of force, and what light horses they have.

To take special note of their buildings, and of the ornaments of their houses within. To take a special note of their apparel and furniture, and of the substance that the same is made of, of which a merchant may make a guess as well of their commodity, as also of their wants. To note their shops and warehouses, and with what commodities they abound, the price also. To see their shambles [slaughterhouses], and to view all such things as are brought into the markets, for so you shall soon see the commodities, and the manner of the people of the inland, and so give a guess of many things. To note their fields of grain, and their trees of fruit, and how they abound or not abound in one and other, and what plenty or scarcity of fish they have.

The true purpose of the voyage tended towards profit rather than enquiry and Hakluyt, at least, seems to have regarded Pet and Jackman as simultaneously managers of a trade fair and travelling salesmen. They were to take with them a vast array of items, not merely to sell them but also to show off the quality of English goods in general.

It is interesting to note, however, that Hakluyt still seems to have regarded wool as the principal commodity that England had to offer. To the extent that this was true it was a sorry state of affairs. English wool had been in decline for over a century and the nation's previous over-reliance on it was serving the people ill. If we look back to the 1300s, we can see Francisco Balducci Pegolotti,[2] a Florentine merchant who certainly visited England and possibly lived there, listing at great length the riches on offer at the markets of Constantinople. They include indigo, wormwood, madder, alum, horse hides, ox hides, buffalo hides, suet in jars, iron of every kind, tin of every kind, lead of every kind, raisins of every kind, soap of Venice, soap of Ancona, soap of Apulia in wooden cases, the soap of Cyprus and of

2. See the Merchant's Tale.

Rhodes in sacks, broken almonds in bags, honey in kegs or skins, cotton wool, rice, dried figs of Majorca and Spain in hampers, safflower, henna, cumin, pistachios, sulphur, senna, pitch, round pepper, ginger, barked brazil wood, lac, zedoary, incense, sugar and powdered sugar of all kinds, aloes of all kinds, quicksilver, cassia fistula, sal ammoniac, cinnabar, cinnamon, galbanum, laudanum of Cyprus, mastic, copper, unwrought amber (big, middling and small), 'stipt' coral, clean and fine coral (middling and small), raw silk, saffron, clove stalks and cloves, cubebs, lignaloes, rhubarb, mace, long pepper, galangal, broken camphor, nutmegs, spike, cardamoms, scammony, pounding pearls, manna, borax, gum Arabic, dragon blood, camel's hay, turbot, silk gauze, sweetmeats, gold wire, dressed silk, wrought amber in beads, buckrams of Erzingan and Cyprus, silk velvets, damasks, maramati, gold cloth of every kind, nachetti and nacchi of every kind, all cloths of silk and gold except gauzes, undressed vairs [squirrel furs], and vair bellies and backs, Slavonian squirrels, martens and fitches, goat skins and ram skins, dates, filberts, walnuts, salted sturgeon tails, salt, oil of Venice, oil of the March, oil of Apulia, oil of Gaeta, wheat and barley, wine of Greece, wine of Turpia in Calabria, wine of Patti in Apulia, wine of Cutrone in Calabria, wine of the March, wine of Crete, and wine of Romania. When he turned to England, however, Pegolotti's interest can be summarized in just that one word: wool.

Two centuries later, though, Hakluyt is still referring to England as 'this clothing realm', asking the two merchants to undertake what in other circumstances would amount to industrial espionage:

> What I would have you there to remember [is] specially what
> excellent dyeing they use in these regions, and therefore to
> note their garments and ornaments of houses: and to see
> their dye houses, and the materials and simples that they use
> about the same, and to bring musters and shows of the
> colours and of the materials, for that it may serve [England]
> to great purpose.

Of course, no language is as dead as yesterday's jargon, and when scanning Hakluyt's list of English commodities the eye stumbles on many unfamiliar items. Kerseys, worsteds, broadcloth, baize, flannel and Spanish blankets are still familiar, at least to specialists, but even with the aid of *The Oxford English Dictionary* it is difficult to rescue frizadoes, carels, Bristol friezes, motleys, woadmols, says and rash from oblivion. Many of the items on the list are, of course, related to cloth and clothing, and the service industry that had arisen out of England's productive capacity: taffeta hats, mariners' caps (one colour: red), shoes of Spanish leather, quilted nightcaps of Levantine taffeta, stockings of kersey, silk and jersey, velvet girdles, silk garters of several kinds, leather girdles, knitted gloves, gloves of leather, perfumed glues, velvet shoes, and slippers. Behind the desire to do business there lay a sense of the social economy of England and, perhaps, the impact of the wool trade's decline so many decades past its zenith. Nothing can be divorced from its place of origin: two of the cloths in the list above, kersey and worsted, take their names from English villages, in Suffolk and Norfolk respectively. Centuries-old communal endeavours were at stake and, certainly, Hakluyt had an eye to the social goods that sales could bring. Six times he drives home the same point: 'finding ample vent of any thing that is to be wrought in this realm, is more worth to our people, besides the gain of the merchant, than Christchurch, Bridewell, the Savoy, and all the hospitals of England'.

Consequently, Jackman and Pet were seemingly to take an extraordinary array of items along with them: pewter bottles, English glass, mirrors for women, combs of ivory, box or horn, linen, knives in their sheaths, silk handkerchiefs, 'glazen eyes to ride with against dust', hourglasses, 'spectacles of the common sort, others of crystal trimmed with silver', silk buttons of every size and colour, needles 'great and small', locks and keys, hinges, bolts and hasps, soap, saffron ('the best of the world'), candles, copper spurs and hawks' bells, a pot of cast iron, all sorts of garden seeds, lead of all kinds, English iron, copper wire, *aqua vitae*, edge tools, and thread. Then there were the items of overstock that Hakluyt, or his patrons, seem simply to have wanted to off-load – red ochre, glue, rolls of parchment – or those for which they presumably had no use, such as brimstone, antimony and black rabbit skins, 'for we abound with the commodity, and may spare it'; or those items over which the air of the kitchen sink seems to hover regarding the decision to recommend them: 'a painted bellows... perhaps they have not the use of them'.

There is also good advice on how to entertain the great and the good on board ship, the best of which, no doubt, was to set the sweetest perfumes beneath the hatches 'to make the place sweet against their coming aboard' – a tall order, one imagines, in the circumstances. For similar reasons, Hakluyt directed that the guests themselves were to be 'besprinkled' with sweet waters the moment they stepped over the gunwale.

To be laid out for the guests' delight were delicacies such as marmalade, figs, the charmingly named sucket (a kind of candied fruit), raisins, damask prunes, dried pears, walnuts, almonds and olives. It was the opposite of the grand banquet, which is food as an expression of power; these were tastes and flavours to tantalize and seduce, small blandishments in place of bluff authority. Among them too were comfits, sugared plums, 'made of purpose by him that is most excellent, that shall not dissolve' and 'the apple-john that endureth two years to make show of our fruits': examples of English husbandry that speak of ingenuity and excellence, of refined, sophisticated tastes to parallel the contemporary vogue for miniatures.

The objects to be taken with the aim of setting the right tone echo the naiveté and otherworldliness that we might more commonly associate with the petty gifts given to Native Americans and other 'savages'. It's difficult not to be reminded of children starting at a new school, out in the playground, keen to impress. Pet and Jackman were to take a coloured map of England – 'one of the biggest sort I mean', interjects Hakluyt, wanting to ensure everything is just so – and a large map of London, with 'the river drawn full of ships of all sorts, to make the more show of your great trade and traffic in trade of merchandise'. It is a nice irony that these maps, drawn to advance trade and mercantilism, were themselves here regarded as a commodity of the highest price: 'If you take Ortelius's book of maps with you... it were not amiss: and if need were, to present the same to the Great Khan, for it would be to a prince of marvellous account.' The Khan,

Hakluyt surmised, would be equally enthralled ('as I persuade myself,' he says, none too authoritatively) by 'the book of the attire of all nations' and 'such books as make show of herbs, plants, trees, fishes, fowls and beasts of [the European] regions'. Perhaps the Khan had been feeling the lack of information about English horticulture – somehow, though, one suspects not. It certainly doesn't seem the case that the people and potentates of the East reciprocated the fascination with which they were regarded by the West. But then, why would they?

The Native's Tale

*A Huron lord makes a mockery
the King of France*

Donnaconna, as he is named in the narratives, was
Lord of Hochelaga, a kingdom of the Huron people
close by the Gulf of St Lawrence. He first met
Jacques Cartier, from St Malo, and his men on 25 July 1534. It was
Cartier's first voyage to the Americas and this was, of course, to his
mind virgin territory: no European had yet set foot there and no one
had any idea what it might contain. Nor surprisingly, while both
groups were cordial, they were also cautious. The men of Hochelaga
kept their womenfolk back, among the trees; the French were concerned about pilfering. Yet there was an accord between them
nonetheless.

The next day Cartier commanded the building of a 30-foot-high cross at the entrance to Gaspé Bay. It was adorned with the three *fleur-de-lys* (the stylized lilies of the French royal arms) and the phrase 'Vive le Roy de France' was carved on it in what Cartier called 'antique letters'. It wasn't long before Donnaconna, who was perhaps in his 50s, and was accompanied by his three grown-up sons and his brother, rowed out to Cartier's ship to remonstrate. Donnaconna made a long speech, none of which was comprehensible to the French. Still, they got the impression that he regarded the cross as a symbol of their attempt to claim the land. In this he was astute, for that was exactly what it was.[1] His arm swept around the bay, as if to say: you cannot claim this land, it is mine. Cartier tried to mollify the king: with hand gestures he tried to convey the idea that the cross was merely a marker to enable the French to find the spot again.

The Huron were brought on board Cartier's ship – it is not clear how willingly – and the French wined and dined them. They assured Donnaconna repeatedly of their good intentions. They plied the Huron with gifts – shirts, coats, red caps, copper neck-chains, a hatchet each, an axe. All seemed amicable at last. The French asked if Donnaconna could leave two of his sons with them[2] and said that they would return soon with more goods to trade. As far as we can tell, Donnaconna assented. Certainly, two of his sons, known to the French as Taignoagny and Dom Agaya, remained on board and sailed to France.

Cartier was as good as his word. On Friday 13 August 1535 he was back in the Gulf of St Lawrence, with the two 'princes' of Hochelaga up on deck, excitedly spying out familiar land. It was at this moment that the name 'Saguenay' first entered the record, as they told Cartier of a great kingdom, two days' journey inland, situated near a lake,

1. The territory named New France. It seems to have escaped everyone's attention that there was already a New France: under this name Verrazzano had claimed virtually the entire coastline north of Florida up to Hudson Bay in 1524. The French court, for reasons known only to itself, was largely uninterested.
2. This was not an exceptional request, although it was more usual to leave the same number of people behind in their stead, primarily as a kind of surety, but also to find out more about customs and culture and so forth.

which today is named (appropriately) Gull Lake.

Donnaconna, for his part, no doubt greeted the return of the French with mixed emotions. He was surely pleased and relieved to see his sons again, but like other Native Americans, or at least those who had welcomed the strangers to their shores on their first meeting, he must have felt that a second meeting was a more ambivalent pleasure. It implied more permanent relations. Visitors are one thing; neighbours are quite another.

If Donnaconna hadn't found out from Taignaogny and Dom Agaya, he would have noticed that Cartier seemed strangely interested in Saguenay. So he and his family told Cartier more about it.

The kingdom, it seemed, was actually rather more than two days' travel away. It was 'more than a moon's journey from the mouth [of the Saguenay River] towards the west-north-west'. However, the river was only navigable in small boats after about eight or nine days. More intriguingly still, Donnaconna said, in Saguenay 'the natives go clothed and dressed in woollens like ourselves,' Cartier reported. 'There are many towns and tribes composed of honest folk who possess great store of gold and copper.'

At this point, Donnaconna managed to suggest yet more opportunities opening up elsewhere for the French. Perhaps he just made a lucky guess, but it seems more likely that he has picked up hints and inferences from Cartier's questioning – Donnaconna was nothing if not wily:

Furthermore, they told us that the whole region from the Saguenay [River] up as far as Hochelaga and the kingdom of the Saguenay is an island which is encircled and surrounded by rivers and by the Saint Lawrence, and that beyond the kingdom of the Saguenay this tributary flows through two or three large very broad lakes until one reaches a fresh-water sea, of which there is no mention of anyone having seen the bounds...

Cartier's mind was no doubt racing at this point. Could this be the Northwest Passage, the sought-after route to far Cathay? Better still, could it connect directly to the Asian landmass? There was much for Cartier to think about here.

In the meantime Donnaconna, just for good measure, tried to entice his visitors with stories of another far-off place. A one-month journey down the St Charles River would, he said, take them

> to a land where ice and snow never come; but in which there are continual wars of one tribe against the other. In that country grow in great abundance oranges, almonds, walnuts, plums and other varieties of fruit. They also told us that the inhabitants of that land were dressed and clothed in furs, like themselves. On inquiring if gold and copper were to be found there they said no... I [Cartier] am of the opinion that this land lies towards Florida.

If at any point Cartier found it suspicious that his host seemed keen to direct his attention elsewhere in North America, then he was too polite to say so.

In any event, in the autumn Cartier and his men sailed upriver to Hochelaga itself, which stood on the site of modern Montreal. Nothing could have whetted his appetite more for further discovery. It was something close to paradise:

> Along both shores we had sight of the finest and most beautiful land it is possible to see, being as level as a pond and covered with the most magnificent trees in the world. And on the banks were so many vines loaded with grapes that it seemed they could only have been planted by husbandmen... [Three days later] We discovered as fine a country and as level a region as one could wish, covered with the finest trees in the world, such as oaks, elms, walnuts, pines, cedars, spruce, ash, boxwood, willows, osiers and, better than all, a great quantity of grape vines, which were so loaded with grapes that the sailors came on board with their arms full of them... There are likewise many cranes, swans, bustards, geese, ducks, larks, pheasants, partridges, blackbirds,

thrushes, turtledoves, goldfinches, canaries, linnets, nightingales, sparrows and other birds – the same as in France and in great numbers.

The people were open and friendly, almost, it seemed, unfallen. Cartier mentions, for instance, that:

we came across five Indians who were hunting for game. They came to meet our boats without fear or alarm, and in as familiar a manner as if they had seen us all their lives, and when our longboats grounded, one of those Indians took [Cartier] in his arms and carried him on shore as easily as if he had been a six-year-old child, so strong and big was he.

And then:

On reaching Hochelaga there came to meet us more than a thousand persons, both men, women and children, who gave us as good a welcome as ever father gave to his son, making great signs of joy... After this they brought us quantities of fish and of their bread, which is made of Indian corn, throwing so much of it into our longboats that it seemed to rain bread... And the women brought their babies in the arms to have the captain and his companions touch them...

It was all – all of it – quite overwhelming.

The French wintered in a fort they built somewhere near the future site of Quebec City. A good number of Cartier's men died; scurvy was rampant. Cartier ordered those of his men who were well enough to bang on the walls of their fort and shout, to give the impression that the company was at full strength and keeping busy. Donnaconna – long absent in the hinterland, much to the suspicion of the French – returned. They wondered whether he might be planning a surprise attack. However, he revealed to them a cure for scurvy, using a drink made from the bark of a particular tree. Even then, the French suspected poison, but a few of them were brave enough, or desperate enough – Cartier had had at least one of the corpses in the fort cut open to examine what the illness was doing – and drank the proffered broth. Within hours they felt better than they had in months. Guards were lowered.

Cartier, for one, had lost whatever critical faculties he may have once possessed. Perhaps Donnaconna saw this as his opportunity to press home his point. Or perhaps he had noticed the Frenchmen's hostility and was seeking means to win their favour again. Whatever his motive – and with winter still working through perhaps he simply had too much time on his hands and a good audience – Donnaconna recalled some more information about Saguenay. He assured Cartier that he had been to the land of the Saguenay himself. There he had seen immense quantities of gold, rubies and other rich things. Its men were as white as Frenchmen and dressed in wool. He has been beyond Saguenay, too, and had visited the land of dwarfs. He had also been to a country where each inhabitants had only one leg. Best of all, he had 'visited another region where the people, possessing no anus, never eat or digest, but simply make water through the penis'.

Cartier could have responded in several ways to these stories. He deduced, quite reasonably, that if he, a Breton seaman, had turned up at the court of King Francis I with tales of men with no anuses, he would be met with ridicule; from the lips of an Indian lord, however, it would be different. In this he showed himself to have, if not common sense, then at least the measure of his king's character. He decided, therefore, 'to take Chief Donnaconna to France, that he might relate and tell the king all he had seen in the West of the wonders of the world'.

This was not what Donnaconna had expected. When he was summoned to the fort, he proved to be wary, keeping one eye anxiously on the woods behind him, ready to run. Taignaogny, in particular, who had had a good year or so to get to know the French on their own soil, counselled caution. The French contrived to kidnap Donnaconna anyway, showing him to his people from the deck of their ship to prove that they had not harmed him. No doubt, too, they offered the same assurances as they had the previous year.

This time, however, things were different. Five years passed before

Cartier returned. We next catch a glimpse of Donnaconna, in action at the French court, in either 1538 or early 1539. He was fluent, plausible and desperate to get home, but he had the king's ear and could do no wrong. At least, so wrote the Portuguese Ambassador, João Fernando Lagarto, to his master King John III, on 22 January 1539:

> The following night [after dessert] the king again examined the charts and conversed more than an hour with me. He showed me two other charts belonging to him – well-painted and illuminated but not very accurate – and he showed me a river in the land of Cod marked out and set down at his request. He has sent there twice, and he has in this matter a great desire and longing, as was clearly shown. But what he says and what he wishes to do in this matter would make men marvel.
>
> He spoke of this to me many times until I seemed to see it with his eyes. He has despatched thither a Breton pilot named Jacques Cartier, who lives in Brittany, in a town called St Malo; and in the two voyages he made thither, on the first he lost two ships out of three and on the second one out of two; but always brought one home.[3] On the last voyage he brought back three Indians, two of whom are dead. The one who is left is king of three or four towns, according to what [Francis] said, for all that I say here I heard from his own lips. And thus he told me that the river he sent to discover he has heard is 800 leagues long. Well up the river there are two falls and he wishes to send two brigantines with the ships, and when the falls are reached the brigantines can be taken overland. Beyond the falls, the King of France says the Indian chief told him, there is a large city called Saguenay, where there are many mines of gold and silver in great abundance, and men who dress and wear shoes like we do; and there is an abundance of clove, nutmeg and pepper. Thus I believe he will again decide to send there a third

---

3. Lagarto, who came from seafaring stock himself, doesn't seem very impressed by this.

time, given his great desire.

He told me that he wished to build a fort well up the
river, on the north side, and that commencing in the summer
in the following year the brigantines may go there to pass the
falls, for in that land the summer is short, and winter long
and exceeding cold; and it is said that down the river are
snow-clad mountains; and the river contains an abundance of
good fish, and at its mouth there are oranges and
pomegranates. And that there are certain animals whose
hides as leather are worth ten cruzados each, and for this sum
they are sold in France and that 10,000 of these skins being
brought they are worth 100,000 cruzados.

[Francis] is also greatly praising of the rich novelty of the
land: there are men who fly,[4] having wings on their arms like
bats, although they fly but little, from the ground to the tree
and from tree to tree to the ground. And the said Jacques
brought to the king a small sample of gold, ten or twelve
stones shaped like small goose quills, and he says it is fine
gold and comes from the said city of Saguenay.

And [the king] asked me what I thought, to which I
replied that spices had never yet been found anywhere but
below the equator or close to it, and that this river of his is in
the Tropic of Cancer, but further north than the distance of
the Tropic of Cancer to the equator, and that it seemed to
me impossible that spices or gold could be found there,
though there might well be silver. He said then that in

4. This seems ridiculous, although not as anatomically challenging as the men with no
anus. There are several records of attempted human flight from the medieval period.
Some time in the 11th century Oliver of Malmesbury, an English Benedictine monk,
built himself some wings and leapt from a tower into the wind, flying some 125 paces
before falling. In 1178 a white-robed Saracen aeronaut whose name has not survived
tried the same trick in Constantinople, jumping from the tower of the Hippodrome,
watched by a horrified yet fascinated Emperor Manuel Comnenos and his guest, the
Sultan. His results were even less successful than Oliver's. Similar stories are told of
Giovanti Dante, an Italian mathematician, and John Damian, Abbot of Tungland and
physician at the court of James IV, King of Scots. Damian is said to have attempted to
fly from the battlements of Stirling Castle.

Hungary there was mine or mines of very fine gold, and that that country was just as cold and more so, for it lies far north of the equator, which is a fact. I replied that it was a rare thing and a great marvel, and not the general rule in all parts of the world.

All these and other things he spoke of on various occasions, and it would become tedious to relate all; and thus he told me that this Indian king spoke strict truth, because he was questioned on coming on board, and the notary took it down[5], and the captain again questioned him at times, and the king also after his arrival, and he always said the same, and he had never been found in error.

And the Indian king says that he with all his people, friends and relatives will help to pass the falls, and to reach the great city of Saguenay in the brigantines, and he will show them the cloves, nutmeg and pepper plants. I said to the king, may [Donnaconna] be not be like him who tempted Christ, saying '*hic omnia tibi dabo*' – I will offer you anything – so as to return to his own land. The king laughed and said that the Indian king was an honest man, and would not act other than he had said.

As will be apparent from the above, no amount of rational nay-saying could dissuade Francis. As a mark of how important Saguenay was to him, he gave command of the principal voyage to colonize it not to the professional seaman Jacques Cartier, who was thus effectively demoted, but to a nobleman, Jean-François de la Roque, Sieur de Roberval. To make the point that Roberval was to be lord of the new dominion, Francis awarded him the extravagant titles of Lord of Norumbega, Viceroy and Lieutenant General in Canada, Hochelaga, Saguenay, Newfoundland, Belle Isle, Carpunt, Labrador, the Great Bay and Baccalaos.

We can reasonably surmise that Cartier was less than happy about this, since he sailed in 1541 without waiting for Roberval. He was

5. That is: he has sworn it before a lawyer. It must be true.

probably wise to do so, in retrospect, since it would take the insolvent Roberval a year to find the money to finance the colonization, something he ultimately contrived to do through a rather successful spree of piracy against the English. Sadly, too, Cartier sailed without Donnaconna, who had died waiting for his voyage home. How, why or where he died we do not know.

Cartier did indeed penetrate the Saguenay River, as far as the impassable Chicoutimi Falls. Some say that he realised at this point the futility of his quest; others that he mistook marcasite for gold, as Raleigh's men would, and, filling his ship with the stuff, fled for home in the belief that he carried with him his fortune. What is certain is that just as he was about to depart from Newfoundland he met Roberval's ships coming the other way. No doubt relations were strained. Cartier expressed his intention to return home. Roberval forbade it and insisted that he stay. Cartier, not a man given to grand-standing, backed down and harboured his ships with those of his commander. After nightfall, however, he gave orders to weigh anchor and quietly slipped away. By the time Roberval woke, Cartier was long gone into the sunrise.

The Lovers' Tales

We consider two stories of love and adversity
on the high seas

The austere and somewhat puritanical Sieur de Roberval, a Protestant, was perhaps a quixotic choice to lead an expedition charged with, among other aims, converting North America to Catholicism, but we will let that pass. Whatever his faults, there was certainly no doubting his moral rigidity.

Roberval's voyage across to New France was straightforward: he headed towards the Straits of Belle Isle. Yet in other respects Roberval's journey, and his companions, were far from normal. Because the aim was to establish a colony, the sailors were accompanied by a mixed bag of noblemen, soldiers and adventurers, and there were women on board too. Indeed, among them was Roberval's own niece, Marguerite, and her nursemaid, Bastienne (also known as Damienne), who served as a chaperone.

It is hardly surprising that, in the close quarters of a 16th-century ship, amid the attendant terrors of the voyage and fears for what might lie beyond landfall, strong attachments should form. Marguerite fell in love with a young gentleman – it has been suggested that she was his reason for embarking in the first place – and Bastienne connived with the two of them to keep the affair secret. Needless to say, secrecy in such a confined and ordered place proved impossible, and towards the end of the voyage the relationship came to the attention of Roberval. He reacted, as a thin-skinned man might to public shame, with pitiless rage.

A little way north of the Straits of Belle Isle, off the coast of Newfoundland – roughly speaking, east of what is now Fox Harbour – was an island known as the Isle of Demons, which had been a fixture on most maps of the coast from the early 16th century. Sailors passing by heard strange unearthly noises, wild and compelling, some of which eerily mimicked the cries of men. André Thevet, in his *Cosmographie Universelle* (1575), says that:

> I myself have heard it, not from one, but from a great number
> of the sailors and pilots with whom I have made many
> voyages, that when they passed this way they heard in the air,
> on the tops and about the masts, a great clamour of men's
> voices, confused and inarticulate.

Here, Thevet says, Roberval set his indiscreet niece on shore, together with Bastienne and four arquebuses for their self-defence. Then he weighed anchor and left.

It isn't hard to imagine what Marguerite and her nurse must have felt, watching helpless as the wind and the waves carried the known world away over the horizon. There was at least one consolation: as Roberval's ship drew away, the two women saw something plunge into the cold Atlantic waters and soon Marguerite's lover could be seen, struggling desperately through the surf to join them, with more guns and ammunition in tow. Roberval had ordered him shackled, but the order had not been carried out.

What kind of life the three of them now led we don't really know in any detail. They built themselves a sturdy hut, fished, hunted and fended for themselves as best they could, lying awake at night dreaming as the sailors did – and, for that matter, Thevet when he came to tell the tale – that the wild winds that tore across the island were demons hungry for their souls.

Marguerite fell pregnant and gave birth. Her baby soon sickened and died, and was laid to rest. Worse, perhaps, her lover soon followed. By now it was winter, and Marguerite and Bastienne could not dig the hard, frozen ground to make a grave. Instead, they kept his cold body in the hut, safe from the island's scavengers, until spring came to loosen the soil. Scenting easy meat, the scavengers still approached; Marguerite kept them at bay with gunshots. Indeed, she shot at least three polar bears, 'white as eggs' she said, who came too close. The following winter Bastienne too passed away and Marguerite was left wholly alone.

Some 30 months after she had been stranded by her uncle the crew of a small French boat, out to fish the rich Newfoundland banks, saw thin smoke trailing out from the island. Their first thought was that, like the demon voices, it must be a lure of the Devil. They kept their distance. Soon, however, curiosity got the better of them and, as they drew slowly closer to shore, they saw what looked like a young woman, wretchedly dressed, waving desperately to them from the shore. Marguerite, at last, was saved.

This story offers many difficulties. The most obvious is that there is no Isle of Demons. Although it survived on maps until the mid-17th century, it disappeared without much of a whimper soon afterwards. However, Jean Alfonse, Roberval's pilot, repeatedly refers in his writings to the Isles de la Demoiselle,[1] just north of Newfoundland – which has been interpreted as a reference to Marguerite's story – and Marguerite's island has also been identified by one authority with Harrington Island.

---

1. These four islands have been identified, I don't know how accurately, as Great Mecatina, Treble Hill, Flat and Murr.

Another difficulty is Thevet. One 20th-century expert character-ized him as 'a congenital liar', but his most recent Canadian editors offer a more nuanced view: that he was 'credulous, egotistical and [merely] something of a liar'. On the other hand, he was a personal friend of both Roberval and Cartier, and the story isn't given at third hand, as tall tales usually are. Thevet claims that he met Marguerite at Natron in Perigord and heard the tale directly from her. She even became something of a celebrity once the story had been spread around. Marguerite de Valois, a sister of King Francis I, used a slight-ly cleaned-up version of it in her collection of stories, the *Heptameron* (1559).

At least one other pair of star-crossed lovers falls within our remit, too, albeit within even less claim to historical accuracy.

The island Madeira was officially discovered by the modern world in 1418 – if 1418 constitutes modern – when a Portuguese sailor, João Gonçalves Zarco, sighted its sister island Porto Santo, having been driven west from Africa by a storm. However, a number of Portuguese sources, including one allegedly written for Zarco's patron, Prince Henry the Navigator, claim that the island was first discovered by an Englishman in the preceding century.

During the reign of Edward III – some say in 1344, others around 1370 – one Robert Macham fled with his mistress Anne D'Arfet, also known as Arabella D'Arcy, from the port of Bristol. Heading for Spain, he ran into a storm and was blown wildly off course; coming to Madeira, he cast anchor in what is now known as the bay of Machico, so named in his honour. Anne had been seasick, so Macham brought some men ashore to look for fresh water and fruit to relieve her. The island, uninhabited at this point, was something of a paradise, a presentiment, perhaps, of the further surprises that the western seas had in store. Hakluyt lists the 'great store of divers sorts of fruits' that grew there: 'pears, apples, plums, wild dates, peaches of divers sorts, melons, batatas [yams], oranges, lemons, pomegranates, citrons, figs, and all manner of garden herbs'.

While Macham and his men were exploring the island, his ship, its remaining crew perhaps uncertain of the unknown harbour, rode further out to sea and Anne, it is said, died of heartbreak at the thought of leaving Macham behind. He built a chapel in her honour, in which to bury her, and had his name carved beside hers on her tombstone.

According to some sources, Macham and his men then made a boat from the trunk of a single tree, and put to sea with neither sail nor oar to steer them. Washing up on the coasts of Africa, they were taken up by the Moors and presented to their king as a thing of wonder. Other sources say that Macham died five days after Anne and was buried alongside her. His men then made it as far as Morocco, where they were enslaved. They told their story to a Spanish pilot called Juan de Morales, who later was himself captured by Zarco. Whatever the truth of it all, this version is certainly neater.

Madeira, like most of the islands of the Atlantic – of which many more were supposed than ever discovered – invited more than its fair share of speculation. (It would be unkind to call it invention.) Hakluyt, for instance, reports claims that between Madeira and the isle of Palma, in the Canaries, is 'an island not yet discovered which is the true island Madera called Saint Brandon'. Which is a reminder of the trail that St Brendan's legendary travels left all over the medieval Atlantic.

Hakluyt also makes claims for an English connection to the Canaries. He quotes at length a description of the islands by one Thomas Nicols, who spent seven years there. Of the island of Hierro, Nicols claims that the only vineyard was planted by a man named John Hill, from Taunton in Somerset. He then adds that Hierro

has no kind of fresh water. But in the middle of the island grows a great tree with leaves like an olive tree, which has a great cistern at its foot. This tree continually is covered with clouds, and by means thereof the leaves of the said tree continually drop water, very sweet, into the said cistern, which comes to the said tree from the clouds by attraction.

In Hakluyt's defence, and as already noted, the islands of the Atlantic have always proved attractive to fantasy. Indeed, in the guise of the Hesperides, or the Fortunate Isles, the Canary Islands long hovered just over the horizon of the western imagination. Solinus, at the end of the classical tradition, describes them as 'withdrawn forty days' sailing into the innermost part of the sea'. Treating each island in turn, he asserts that 'in one, called Ombrion, there are reeds the size of trees; the black reeds yield a bitter drink but the white a sweet one… In another, Nivaria, it is permanently snowing'; and in Canaria there are 'dogs of exceeding hugeness'. In general, though, says Solinus, the Hesperides are misnamed, since the sea throws the carcasses of monstrous beasts up on to the shore to rot, and they 'infect all things with a horrible stench'.

The Amazons' Tales

*We ponder the peripatetic career
of the female warrior race*

The Amazons have been with us a long time, but they have proved remarkably reluctant to let themselves get pinned down. Herodotus, for instance, places them six days' journey to the northeast of the river Tanaïs, which we know as the Don, in Scythia, where it flows into the Sea of Azov.

The 11th-century German historian Adam of Bremen, in contrast, has them on the northern shores of the Baltic, somewhere in the Gulf of Bothnia:

Some assert that they conceive by drinking water. Others, however, say that they become pregnant through intercourse with seafaring merchants, or with their own prisoners, or with other monsters which are not rare in those parts; which appears to us more credible. If their offspring are of the male sex, they are cynocephali [literally, dog-headed]; but if of the female, beautiful women. These women live together and despise fellowship with men, whom indeed they repulse in manly fashion, if they come. Cynocephali are those who have their heads in their breast; in Russia they are often to be seen as prisoners, and their speech is a mixture of talking and barking.

The City of Women, as described by the 13th-century Arab author Qazwini, was on an unnamed island to the south of China, yet it is also clearly drawn from the same tradition:

Its inhabitants are women [who] ride horses and themselves wage war. They show great bravery in conflict. They also have slaves. Every slave in turn visits his mistress at night, remains with her all night, rises at dawn and goes out secretly at daybreak. If then one of them gives birth to a boy, she kills him on the spot…

Qazwini adds, just in case we might be unsure, that its existence 'is a fact of which there is no doubt'.

Marco Polo takes things still further and is yet more specific. He tells a story about two islands, called, helpfully, Male and Female. The men, as you might expect, live alone on Male island for nine months of the year. However, every March they decamp to Female for three months, to live with their wives. If the women bear children, the boys live with their mothers until they are 14, at which point they are dispatched to Male, while the girls, of course, stay on Female permanently. The Male island, in Polo's telling, is the more pleasant. Fine ambergris washes ashore on its beaches and the men catch great fish from the sea, some of which they trade. They live on a diet of meat, milk and rice. The people on both islands are Christian, but adhere to the Old Testament. They come within the archdiocese of

Socotra, itself an island of pearl-fishers, frankincense and myrrh.

Depending on how one interprets Polo's directions, Male and Female are among either the five islands of Khuryia Muriya, off the coast of Oman and now barely inhabited, or the islands of the Yemenite archipelago, which includes Abd Al-Kuri and Socotra. Alternatively, if one takes his description of them as sitting in the ocean 500 miles south of Makran, a region located where Pakistan now abuts Iran, then they don't exist at all. Yet one 15th-century mapmaker, Fra Mauro, gives the islands names – Mangla and Nebila – though he places them to the south of Zanzibar.

So much for Amazons in the Old World. In the New World, Columbus was told by some Native Americans that Martinique

> had no inhabitants but women, who at a certain time of the year were visited by the Cannibals (Caribs); if the children born were boys they were brought up and sent to their fathers, if girls they were retained by the mothers. They reported also that these women had certain subterranean caverns in which they took refuge if any one went thither except at the established season.

And, as we shall see, there will be further encounters with them in South America, where they will find a permanent home.

The Merchant's Tale

A medieval trader offers some much-needed advice about the road to Cathay

If ever anyone needed an example of a vanished world, they need look no further than the medieval trade routes from the Mediterranean to the East. It is not just that many of the cities have fallen into ruin, and that their former wealth and position are unimaginable; it is also that a whole complex economy that survived – indeed thrived – for centuries, even millennia, has been obliterated. It was the principal artery of world trade, the only means of transporting goods from one end of the known world to the other. Now these places are all but invisible in the eyes of the world. How much, for instance, do most people in the West know about Mongolia, or Uzbekistan or the rest of Central Asia, even now?

We should perhaps be thankful, then, that the obliging 14th-century merchant Francisco Balducci Pegolotti wrote a 'How to...' book on the subject of one of these particular routes, called *Pratica della Mercatura*. Not much is known about Pegolotti. His book dates from around 1340 and only one copy of the manuscript is believed to have survived. All that we know is that he was a Florentine who spent some time in Antwerp, London and Cyprus.

Pegolotti begins his advice for those who wish to reach what he calls Camalec[1] – modern-day Beijing – at a starting point on the edge of Christian Europe: Tana, which is now known as Azov,[2] on the banks of the river Don. Tana, like Caffa,[3] is a forgotten colony. Like Caffa, too, it was Genoese, having been taken over by the Italian city-state some 20 years before Pegolotti produced his work. Its roots were ancient, however. Tanaïs had been an established Greek colony as far back as 600 BC. It was, for the Greeks, something like the principal boundary of their world; beyond was Scythia, six days' journey into which from Tanaïs brought travellers into Amazon country, or so said Herodotus.[4] Two thousand years later things weren't that different: this was still a stepping-off point, the beginning of the unknown.

From Tana, Pegolotti advises merchants to head for Gintarchan, which is Astrakhan on the Volga. However, this is not today's city of the same name, which lies on the Volga delta, more than 50 miles from the Caspian Sea, though it is a major port nonetheless. This earlier Astrakhan was further upriver, but it was sacked and razed to the ground by Tamerlane in the winter of 1395. It was, says our guide, a 25 days' journey from Azov with an ox-wagon, but ten to twelve days with a horse wagon. For the most part the way lay across low, open grasslands, in places barely rising above sea level, bordering on desert scrub in parts.

This was the least safe part of the journey, although Pegolotti is

1. Marignolli in the Legate's Tale would call it Cambaleth. Both names derive from the Mongol *Khan-Balik*, 'city of the ruler'.
2. By the time the Mercator-Hondius Atlas came along, at the turn of the 16th and 17th centuries, it was already known in German as 'Aßow'.
3. See the Legate's Tale.
4. See the Amazons' Tales.

vague on the subject. 'Even when this part of the road is at its worst,' he says, 'if you have some sixty men in the company you will go as safely as if you were in your own house.' He doesn't mention what would happen if there were 59 or fewer, but presumably personal safety was also the reason why he strongly advises that 'you must let your beard grow long and not shave'. There were plenty of 'Moccols' – Mongol or Tartar bandits – on the road, although Pegolotti doesn't specifically say that it was they who posed the threat. He was not as helpful as he might have been.

Nevertheless, anyone who spends any time with Pegolotti will be struck by the diligence and enthusiasm with which he enumerates and details the dizzying variety of customs duties that his fellow merchants were relieved of everywhere they passed. He was not a man to whom the loss of money was anything other than an indignity. It is thus all the more noticeable that he recommends that no expense be spared at Tana in hiring a dragoman, or interpreter. 'You must not try to save money in the matter of dragomen by taking a bad one instead of a good one,' he insists, no doubt knowing his readers' predilections well. 'The additional wages of the good one will not cost you so much as you will save by having him.' In addition, one is adjured to hire 'two good men servants' who speak the language.

Female company was optional. In a curious observation Pegolotti notes that 'if the merchant likes to take a woman with him from Tana, he can do so; if he does not like to take one there is no obligation' – for all the world as if there were places where such things *were* compulsory. He adds, somewhat earnestly, that a man who took a woman along would be kept more comfortably.

Pegolotti was quite cavalier about provisions. This was a major trade route and, at least according to his book, there was no shortage of food, especially meat. All one needed to take was enough flour and salt fish for the number of days' journey he recommended.

From Astrakhan it was a mere day's journey upriver to Sarai,[5] the western capital of the Mongol empire and home to the Kipchak

---

5. There was a contemporary rumour, which Pegolotti doesn't mention, that Job was buried in Sarai. As with the tomb of Abraham for which Coryat searched in vain, there seemed to be a need to seed the alien east with familiar Christian landmarks.

Khanate, otherwise known as the Golden Horde. This city, like Astrakhan, was to be levelled by Tamerlane in 1395; unlike Astrakhan, however, Sarai was never rebuilt. From there it was a further eight days, either by water – presumably back down the Volga delta and east along the shore of the Caspian Sea – or else overland, to Saracanco, or Sarachik, on the lower reaches of the Ural River, another city that no longer exists. The water route, says Pegolotti, was preferable: merchants were taxed less on their goods.

From Saracanco it was 20 days' travel in a camel wagon to Organci, which straddled the River Oxus, now generally called the Amu Darya (Amu River). This was not the modern city of Urgench in Uzbekistan. Organci/Urgench had been ravaged, in 1221, and then rebuilt by Genghis Khan, and in Pegolotti's day it was the capital city of a region called Khwarezm, which until fairly recently had been independent of the Mongol khans. It was also more or less on the border of the lands under the sway of the Golden Horde. The people abandoned the city in the 17th century when the river changed its course; the new city is some 60 miles to the southeast of the site of the old. That Organci was, according to Pegolotti, an excellent market for western goods, particularly for Genoese or Venetian linen.

The next part of the journey was a bleak 35- or 40-day trek by camel train across the Kyzylkum Desert, through what are now Uzbekistan and western Kazakhstan, to Oltrarre, or Otrár, on the Syr River, near modern Shimkent. It had been the first of Genghis Khan's western conquests. (Tamerlane died here on 17 February 1405, while en route to China. His body was embalmed and returned to Samarkand.)

Here, though, Pegolotti's trail becomes somewhat hard to follow. What he says is that the journey with pack-asses from Oltrarre to Armalec took 45 days and that on every one of those days travellers would encounter Moccols on the road. The question is, where was Armalec? There is indeed an Olmaliq a little south-southeast of Tashkent, but that does not solve the problem. In the first place, 45 days is rather a long time to tackle what looks like a relatively short distance. The second and insuperable difficulty, however, is that this Olmaliq was established as recently as 1951. The name means 'apple grove'; there clearly must once have been another. The answer seems to be – not that there's much consensus on the subject – that it was another name for Kuldja, or Yining, on the Ili River, which falls out of Tian Shan, the celestial mountains. This city at least has the advantage of having been called Almarikh in the 13th century, which is close enough, although trying to guess how a Florentine might have chosen to transcribe a Mongol or Chinese place name 660-odd years ago – even assuming that the name hasn't changed in the intervening period and that the town or city still exists – is hardly what you could call a precise science.

One of the surprises about this identification is that this city did not lie on one of the more usual 'silk routes' between East and West. A more common route would have been south from Otrar to the Fergana Valley, which is fed by the Oxus, and is still rich in both silk and cotton, before heading east through one of the more accessible passes in the Fergana Mountains to Kashgar, on the edge of the formidable Takla Makan desert.

Pegolotti's merchant would have found himself northeast of there, having either crossed or skirted the low black mountains of Karatau in what is now southern Kazakhstan and then headed east through the valley of the Ile River, which, although relatively fertile, is nonetheless rugged, challenging country. From here there was little choice: presumably the idea was to loop around to the north of the Po-lo-K'o-Nu Mountains, before coming back to the oasis at Turfan. Perhaps that wasn't bad advice. The more traditional silk routes required travellers to edge from oasis to oasis around either the northern or southern perimeter of the Takla Makan, one of the driest and least hospitable areas on the planet.

Although Pegolotti is silent on the subject, the obvious choice was to follow the paths down the Kansu corridor, the 600-mile-long bottleneck through which most such caravans passed on their way to or from eastern China. It's not entirely clear that this is what Pegolotti recommended, but logic suggests that there was no other practical route to take, unless one wanted to take on the massive barrier of the Kunlun Mountains to the south.

In any event, the next marker that Pegolotti mentions lay a full

70 days' journey with pack-asses from Armalec, at a place that Pegolotti calls Camexu. The favoured identification for this is Kan-chou, in southwestern China. There is nothing implausible about this, but there will certainly have been cities along the way, most obviously Lan-chou on the Huang-ho River at the southern end of the Kansu corridor, which, assuming that Pegolotti came that way, he would have found impossible to miss.

From Camexu to Cassai, the next stop on Pegolotti's itinerary, took not many more than 45 days on horseback, with a short river journey at the end. We will meet Cassai again, since it is Marignolli's Campsay, now Hang-Chou. Less easily impressed than either Marignolli or Marco Polo, Pegolotti describes it as 'a most active place of business'. Indeed, the arduousness of the journey can be deduced from the fact that business – the whole point of the exercise, after all – hasn't been mentioned since Organci, some 200 days' trav-el earlier. Here merchants were required to convert their silver coins into paper currency, called *balishi*, something of a novelty for anyone from the West. It was made of yellow paper and stamped with the imperial seal. 'All the people of the country are bound to receive it. And yet you shall not pay a higher price for your goods because your money is of paper,' notes Pegolotti, struck with wonder at the idea of such a thing. (When Marco Polo told fellow Venetians about *balishi* they regarded it as a Mandevillean flight of fancy and further proof that he had invented the whole narrative of his travels.)

Journey's end was now just 30 days away, at Cambaleth (or Camalec), 'a great resort of merchants, and in which there is a vast amount of trade,' says Pegolotti, gleefully. Indeed, he adds, the whole journey was 'perfectly safe, whether by day or night'. There is one caveat, though: if a merchant died on the road, all his goods would be seized by the lord of the country where he had died – unless, that is, one of his companions pretended to be his brother, in which case the property would go to him. That's not exactly a cheery thought, or necessarily one to inspire friendship and loyalty on the long road from the West, but it was another of Pegolotti's practical considera-tions, nonetheless.

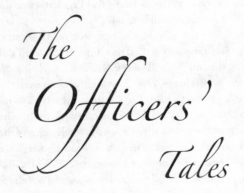

The Officers' Tales

*A naval officer makes the worst
mistake of his career, and an American explorer
discovers the meaning of folly*

The Northwest Passage – the elusive sea-route to the riches of the east over the top of North America – was still in
vogue in the early 19th century, with good reason.
Conditions in the sub-Arctic waters were more favourable than they
had ever been, thanks to several years of freakish weather. As
William Scoresby the Younger, a whaling captain, had written to Sir
Joseph Banks, President of the Royal Society, regarding a voyage he
had made in 1817: 'about 2,000 square leagues [18,000 square miles]
of the surface of the Greenland seas were perfectly void of ice, all of
which had disappeared within the last two years'.

One year later an up-and-coming naval officer, John Ross, was offered the chance to lead an expedition through just these waters in search of the Northwest Passage. There's little doubt from Ross's account that we are now very much in the age of science. Ross was instructed to pay close attention to 'the variation and inclination of the magnetic needle, and the intensity of the magnetic force'. He was to 'endeavour to ascertain how far the needle may be affected by the atmospherical electricity, and what effect may be produced on the electrometer and magnetic needle on the appearance of the aurora borealis'. He was also to 'keep a correct register of the temperature of the air and of the surface of the sea, in various situations, and at different depths'. And he was to 'cause the dip of the horizon to be frequently observed… and ascertain what effect may be produced by measuring that dip across fields of ice, as compared with its measurement across the open surface of the sea'. He had also to observe 'what effect may be produced by observing an object, either celestial or terrestrial, over a field of ice, as compared with objects observed over a surface of water; together with such other meteorological remarks as you have the opportunity of making'. Further, he was to 'attend particularly to the height, direction and strength of the tides, and to the set and velocity of the currents; the depth and soundings of the sea, and the nature of the bottom'.

If this seems repetitive, it is only a very small selection of Ross's instructions, which stretch monotonously for page after page, the tone of each that of a stern schoolmaster to an unpromising pupil. Ross may well have said to himself: all that *and* discover something that has eluded some of Britain's greatest seamen for 200 years? He was, indeed, on a tight leash:

> You are on no account to remain on this service so long,
> unless accidentally caught by the ice, as to be obliged to
> winter on any part of the eastern coast of America or the
> western coast of old Greenland, or the intermediate islands;
> but to leave the ice about the middle or 20th of September,
> or the 1st of October at the latest.

Yet for all the talk of hydrography and meteorological phenomena, it is hard to dispel the feeling that, underneath it all, this was really just a boys' adventure. Certainly one might think so faced with the Admiralty's 'desire that you do, frequently after you have passed the latitude of 65 degrees north... throw overboard a bottle, closely sealed, and containing a paper stating the date and position at which it is launched'.

Sadly, for Ross at least, his expedition is noteworthy for the worst possible reason: the vast question mark over what he actually claimed to have discovered. In A *Voyage of Discovery*, the unfortunately titled book he wrote on his return, there is an engraving of the view from the deck of his ship, HMS *Isabella*, across Lancaster Sound at 3.15 pm on 31 August 1818. Bookended by Cape Castlereagh on the left and Cape Warrender on the right, the illustration is dominated by the white mass of the Croker Mountains at its centre, rising blankly above Cape Rosomond in the foreground. It was drawn by Ross himself – and it illustrates perfectly the problem.

The previous day, 30 August, had been, Ross thought, particularly fine and pregnant with excitement. In the evening the crew had seen their first star in 12 weeks; it was Capella, the double star. The snowy mountains on either side of what they thought was a strait, clear of cloud at last, reflected innumerable shades of soft colour in the sunlight. The snowless lowlands seemed almost hospitable, and with the evening came warmer weather, calmer waters and the dying away of the wind. 'For the first time,' Ross reported, 'we discovered that the land extended from the south two thirds [of the way] across this apparent strait'. However, continual fog made more detail impossible to clarify.

On board the expedition's two ships the men had debated whether Lancaster Sound was an inlet, or a strait that might lead to the Pacific. One of Ross's men, Captain Sabine, effectively the expedition's scientific officer, was, Ross said, particularly adamant that there was 'no indication of a passage'. He pointed to the lack of a current and the absence of driftwood; as they sailed on, the sea became colder. There were plenty, though, who disagreed, and 'the masthead and crow's nest were crowded with those who were most anxious'.

The following morning, just before 4 am, the officers of the watch woke Ross to tell him that they could see land ahead. By the time he had struggled up on deck, however, the fog had descended again. Nevertheless, Ross thought that he could make out 'a high ridge of mountains, extending directly across the bottom of the inlet. This chain appeared extremely high in the centre, and those towards the north had, at times, the appearance of islands, being insulated by the fog at their bases.' Perhaps at this point Ross was tempted to give up, but, as he says, 'although a passage in this direction appeared hopeless, I was determined completely to explore it and therefore continued all sail'.

That afternoon a similar pattern recurred. At 3 pm the officers of the watch summoned Ross from his dinner because the sky seemed to be clearing. As Ross reported later:

> I immediately therefore went on deck, and soon after it
> completely cleared for about ten minutes and I distinctly saw
> the land, round the bottom of the bay, forming a connected
> chain of mountains with those which extended along the
> north and south sides... I also saw a continuity of ice
> extending from one side of the bay to the other...

Ross named the range he had identified Croker's Mountains, after his employer, the Secretary to the Admiralty, John Wilson Croker.[1]

It seems peculiar that none of the other senior officers roused themselves from the dining table. This was, after all, the high-water mark of their voyage; although they continued to gather scientific data – and no doubt lobbed bottles into the sea as requested – they searched no further for the Northwest Passage. It also appears that by the time they returned to London some of them were having severe

---

1. Whether Croker found this humiliating is anyone's guess. He wasn't a man famed for his sense of humour. It was he who penned the vitriolic review of 'Endymion' in the *Quarterly Review* that, according to the likes of Shelley and Byron at any rate, helped to kill John Keats. And if that review is anything to go by, he wouldn't have been shy about stating his opinions to Ross. Certainly, he didn't seem to regard the fact that he had read no more than a quarter of Keats's poem as a reason to inhibit his criticism.

doubts about Ross's judgement. Indeed, when Ross published his account of the voyage, quoted above, Sabine in particular was indignant, so much so that he dashed off a pamphlet on the subject that, while allowing for decorum and deference to a senior officer, nevertheless shreds both Ross and his judgement.

It seems that Ross had made a particular mistake in trying to bind Sabine to his cause. Sabine seethed:

> In Captain Ross's account of his proceedings in Lancaster's Sound my name is twice introduced, obviously for the purpose of supporting the propriety of his conduct in not prosecuting the examination of the inlet; the inferences which are designed to be conveyed being that he consulted with me and that my opinion coincided with his... Although my opinion was not asked... I should not have noticed the statement if it were a just one; but it is not so.

The impression one gets from Ross's account of the voyage is of a certain collegiality aboard the two ships. According to Sabine, nothing of the sort was the case:

> An importance is here attached to my opinion which did not show itself at the time, nor during the voyage. Captain Ross was accustomed to act solely from his own judgement, he formed his plans and executed them without a reference to any person; he certainly at no time placed his confidence in me; he never showed me his instructions; consequently, I need hardly add that he never consulted my as to his conduct under them.

One can understand Sabine's indignation. According to his version of events, Ross was quoting statements that he had made as if they were authoritative, considered judgements, instead of what they actually were, snippets of casual conversation as the ships approached Lancaster Sound:

The expressions which Captain Ross has recorded as having been used by me before we entered the sound, even if admitted, can have nothing to do with his conduct when in the sound the following evening. All [the] remarks being facts, it is equally possible that I may have made them, as it is certain that the facts are in themselves unimportant… To what do the expressions amount? To the absence of certain indications which every person knows are not conclusive, and to the speculations of an individual before the ships had even entered the Inlet!

It was, of course, Ross's judgement once they were in Lancaster Sound that was really in Sabine's sights. It appears that the reason neither Sabine nor other senior officers such as William Parry had come up onto the deck to see Croker's Mountains is that Ross didn't tell them. Nor did he inform them of his decision to turn the ship around and leave the sound without further exploration. The first time Sabine heard of Captain Ross's decision was some four hours after it had been made. The officer of the watch came down into the gun room, where Sabine was sitting, at around 7 pm and dropped into the conversation the fact that the ships were making all sail out of the inlet. One senses a silence at this point, followed by splutters of indignation from Sabine. He asked why. The officer answered flatly: 'The Captain says he saw land when we were at dinner.' It doesn't sound like a ringing endorsement of the captain's judgement.

Sabine apparently made no effort to hide his feelings on the subject. They probably weren't assuaged by the fact that it wasn't until the next day that he was allowed an opportunity to talk to Ross about what had happened. Lest anyone think that Ross's style of leadership was taking a more consultative tack here, Sabine spells out the situation:

The purpose of this conversation was not to consult about quitting a sound which we had already left; it was not to inquire whether I thought Captain Ross had done right or wrong in leaving it; it was not to learn whether I agreed with

Captain Ross that a passage could not exist, because he well knew that I had not seen the continuity of land, the only decisive proof... The conversation alluded to was occasioned by my very visible mortification at having come away from a place which I considered as the most interesting in the world for magnetic observations, and where my expectations had been raised to the highest pitch, without having had an opportunity of making them.

Ross did, however, explain why they had left. The apparent existence of Croker's Mountains was one reason. Tellingly, perhaps, an unwillingness to risk 'such bad sailing ships so late in the season' was another – strangely absent from Ross's own account of his thinking. It is equally unfortunate that Ross omitted to mention the 'continuity of ice across the bay' as another factor here. Sabine declared:

Had this been mentioned in our conversation on the 1st of September, it would have been unnecessary to have assigned any other reasons for not having gone on. I am quite sure that Captain Ross did not tell me of it, because I was ignorant even after our return to England of there having been ice in Lancaster Sound. Had such a circumstance been mentioned on the voyage, it could not have failed to have struck me as a contradiction to the general conversation and belief.

Sabine doesn't come out and say so, but, clearly, he thought that Ross had realized that he had made a colossal mistake in Lancaster Sound and, with many weeks to reflect on the matter as they sailed home, had conjured up further spurious reasons to support his decision.

It can't have been a happy voyage homewards. Assuming that Sabine's account is reliable, the subject of what their captain had actually seen that afternoon in Lancaster Sound was the talk of the two ships. 'I could not learn that any other person than Captain Ross had professed to have seen the land,' Sabine reports, not without a certain satisfaction.

One feels a certain sympathy for Ross at this point: he was being patronized and hectored by his superiors, challenged by his peers, and doubted by his inferiors. Certainly the balance of power between a captain and his crew had always been a perilous one, particularly on ambitious voyages such as this. One thinks of Raleigh lying to his men about the distance they would travel up the Orinoco, ultimately unwilling to push them on towards El Dorado for fear of revolt. Or of Henry Hudson, the discoverer of Hudson Bay, who was set adrift in the bay, together with his son and a couple of loyal crewmen, with no warm clothes and nothing but a kettle to keep them alive, having asked too much of his men for too long: they were never seen again. The introduction of scientific rigour had done nothing to bolster the captain's authority. Gone were the days when a captain could rely on the ignorance of his men to effect his will, as Verrazzano did, brilliantly, in a voyage of 1527. He was sailing out of Dieppe bound for Brazil, where he was contracted to collect a cargo of dye-wood and return to France. Somewhere off the Cape Verde islands the crews on two of his ships mutinied and demanded to return home. It seems evident from what followed that Verrazzano must have been a man of considerable charm – not to mention guile. He acquiesced in the mutineers' demands immediately, but nevertheless contrived to sail on to Brazil and collect the cargo as contracted before sailing for France, without his men being any the wiser.

To return to poor Captain Ross, Sabine ultimately lays before the public his reservations in full:

> Of Captain Ross's conduct I did not judge, because I did not know what his orders were; but presuming that the object of the voyage was to ascertain whether there was or was not a north-west passage, I considered direct and absolute proof of the continuity of land as the only decisive evidence of its impossibility, and as the evidence which the public would expect.
>
> On Captain Ross's account of the land, therefore, which was the only one I could obtain, I could form but one opinion, that where so much hope had been excited, land

seen for a short time, by a single individual, at a very considerable distance, on a very unfavourable day, and which did not fill up the inlet by so large a space, would not be considered as decisive evidence on our return.

Even when he related [his observations] to me, I did not think them conclusive and the more I considered them, the more strong my conviction grew that Lancaster Sound would be revisited.

This may appear prescient, but things had moved quickly back in London and a second voyage to Lancaster Sound was already being prepared, this time under the leadership of William Parry, not yet 30, who had also served under Ross. Parry's two ships, the *Hecla* and the *Griper*, left England on 11 May 1819. On board again was Captain Sabine, together with some other veterans of the Ross debacle. Parry was too much of a gentleman to say so, but it seems more than likely that among the emotions experienced by his men as they made their way up Lancaster Sound again was a certain *Schadenfreude*. Parry wrote later:

It is more easy to imagine than to describe the almost breathless anxiety which was now visible in every countenance while, as the breeze increased to a fresh gale, we ran quickly up the sound. The mastheads were crowded by officers and men during the whole afternoon, and an unconcerned observer, if any could have been unconcerned on such an occasion, would have been amused by the eagerness with which the various reports from the crow's nest were received all, however, hitherto favourable to our most sanguine hopes.

This time, the sea and sky both stayed clear, and there was little ice to impede their passage. Sure enough, Parry's ships sailed past Ross's point of return, the men observing, no doubt with quiet satisfaction, that the shores remained resolutely distant from each other. Ross's mountain range, on which he had ventured his reputation – as almost everyone but him seems to have suspected – had been nothing but low-lying clouds.

And if anyone were looking for proof of the the idea that history repeats itself, they need look no further than Robert E. Peary, the American Arctic explorer, usually if not incontrovertibly credited with being the first man to reach the North Pole.[2] In June 1906 he could be found on Ellesmere Island, the northernmost part of North America and further north than the current magnetic north. He was looking out northwest across the pack ice, the broken surface of the Arctic Ocean. He was enthralled to see through his binoculars 'the white summits of a distant land'. He reckoned that this vast new island was some 120 miles offshore. With a fine sense of history he named it 'Crocker Land'. In theory this was in honour of one of his expedition's backers; it is tempting, though, to imagine that there might have been some ironic nod to Ross's 'Croker's Mountains' of the previous century.

If so, it would prove doubly ironic. In 1913 an expedition led by Donald Macmillan, who had served under Peary on the expedition that had taken him to the North Pole in 1909, went in search of Crocker Land. Macmillan and his companions set out across the frozen sea from Cape Thomas Hubbard on the northern tip of Axel Heiberg Island, among what are now known as the Queen Elizabeth Islands. On their arduous journey across the polar ice they caught odd glimpses of the valleys and tall mountains of Peary's new landmass.[3] However, they noted that it seemed to change in size and extent depending on the position of the sun in the sky; at certain times it disappeared altogether. After some days' travelling they checked their position on the disorienting ice. They were some 150 miles northwest of Cape Thomas Hubbard and well onto the polar ice cap. To their horror, they realized that, if Peary was correct, they ought to be about 30 miles inland. Turning back downhearted, they sledded their way to the point from which Peary had made his sighting. Sure

---

2. One recent historian has described Peary as 'probably the most unpleasant man in the annals of polar exploration'.

3. The Inuit who accompanied them were, reportedly, unimpressed.

enough there were the mountains and valleys again, caught in the low sunlight. 'There was land everywhere!' they recalled. 'Had we not just come from far over the horizon, we would have returned to our country and reported land as Peary did.'

As tricks of the light go, this one proved particularly costly. Macmillan's expedition, which stretched over a number of years, reportedly cost his backers the extraordinary sum of US$100,000 by the time he made it back home.

The Balloonist's Tale

Three men in a balloon
make an assault upon the North Pole

*I*t seemed obvious, or at least it did to the Norwegian Salomon August Andrée. There he was, at the last gasp of the 19th century, with the North Pole and the Arctic interior still unconquered. Here, too, was a certain technology, not new, but increasingly sophisticated, that would allow people to penetrate the very heart of that interior and reach the Pole itself, in something approaching comfort and ease. The technology he had in mind was the balloon. As he asked one audience:

Has the time not come to revise this question from the very

beginning and to see if we do not possibly possess any other means than the sledge for crossing these tracts? Yes, the time for doing so has certainly come, and we need not search very long before we find a means which is, as it were, created just for such a purpose. The means is the air balloon. Not the dreamed of, perfectly steerable air balloon – so devoutly longed for since we have not yet seen it – but the air balloon which we already possess and which is regarded so unfavourably because attention is paid merely to its weak point...

That weak point was the difficulty of steering, but more of that later.

Whatever else Andrée was, he doesn't seem to have been a dreamer. He had been calm and practical his whole life; even as a child, when he had exhibited a mulish self-assurance, it had been the working of things that interested him. But then his parents had the often-caricatured 19th-century belief that what they called coddling and indulgence would be the ruin of their children. In later life some of Andrée's friends remarked on his endless capacity for self-control; his closest friends, though, saw someone more boyish, jovial and playful. 'There is in our days only one way of retaining a belief in ideal efforts,' he said, 'and that is by endeavouring to make them oneself.'

In 1894 Andrée turned 40. He was working in the Swedish Patent Office, but he was also busy raising funds for his expedition. More than that, he was experimenting with steerage systems for balloons, primarily using drag lines, together with an adjustable sail. The results were impressive, sometimes allowing him to change the balloon's direction by as much as 40 degrees. In this, as in all things, he was clear about what he wanted and set about procuring it. He wanted a gondola beneath the balloon with warm berths for three people; it needed to be seaworthy; it had to have a dark room. He wanted sledges, a canvas boat, guns and ammunition, and enough provisions for four months.

Despite such precautions, he also believed that, with good weather, an expedition could get from Spitzbergen to the Bering Straits –

that is, across the Polar ice cap – in just six days.[1] The balloon he had in mind could fly for 30 days. Sometimes, perhaps with a dash of bravado, he claimed that it would be possible for the balloon to be at the Pole in ten hours. To suggestions that the balloon could be hampered by rain and ice, he replied that it could still fly even if rainfall were many times the seasonal average. He was a practical man and had examined the data; his confidence was absolute.

It was also infectious. So it was that at 6 pm on 18 May 1897 Andrée and his fellow balloonists left Gothenburg harbour in the *Svenskund*, a ship supplied by the Swedish government, headed for Spitzbergen. The companions Andrée had chosen were Nils Strindberg, aged 24, a photographer but also a scientist and physicist – and a relative of the playwright – who was engaged to be married; and Knut Fraenkel, 27, an aspiring adventurer and sportsman, but by trade a civil engineer, whose principal regret in life had been that ill health had left him incapable of following in his father's footsteps into a military career. Fraenkel's qualifications weren't particularly apparent, but Andrée liked him, and that was that.

They stayed in Virgo harbour on Spitzbergen for several weeks. The balloon had to be filled and then they had to wait for the weather to be just right. It was not until 11 July that it turned in their favour. Early in the morning a wind from the south-southwest began to ruffle the still waters of the harbour; by sunrise it was blowing strongly. The sky was clear, save for a few clouds scudding across from the south. Andrée came ashore from the *Svenskund*. He was excited but unsure and wanted to think further. Nevertheless, he ordered the support team to make things ready. Strindberg hurriedly finished a letter to his fiancée in Stockholm.

When he consulted his companions Andrée found Strindberg keen but Fraenkel evasive and unwilling to commit himself to an opinion. Eventually, however, he agreed. They ate breakfast. Andrée asked them again if they were ready. Yes, they were: this was it. Final

---

1. Andrée's great Norwegian compatriot, Fritjof Nansen, had recently attempted to claim the Pole by allowing his boat to drift with the pack ice. He had, incredibly, survived an entire winter in the Arctic, slowly discovering that his theory was wrong.

preparations were made. Everything was double-checked and the guidelines were laid out along the ground to the east of the balloon, each section screwed tightly into the next. Strindberg, still thinking of his beloved Anna, asked a member of the ship's crew to pass his love back to her in person.

The three balloonists entered the gondola at 1.43 pm. Three minutes later the balloon rose from the housing in which it had been sheltered. They had christened it the *Eagle*. Three heavy knives were held in three hands, waiting for the order. 'Cut!', Andrée shouted, and the ropes fell away. Cheers were raised, both on the ground and in the air, for old Sweden. The airmen were elated, almost drunk with pride and wonder at the sensation of flight and at the heroic prospect before them.

The *Eagle* rose slowly to 300 feet, heading, as it should, northeast across the harbour, the guidelines raking through the waves beneath. Halfway across, however, something went wrong. The balloon was sinking rapidly, so much so that the gondola smacked into the water. Andrée, Strindberg and Fraenkel quickly threw out eight bags of ballast, and the gondola seemed to jerk itself free of the sea as the balloon began to rise again. At some point in the midst of all this Strindberg made time to jot down a quick card to his lover.

But all was not well. One of the men realized the significance of the jerk they had experienced in the harbour: they had left the bottom two thirds of their guidelines behind them in the sea. They must have become twisted when they were laid out on the ground and been unscrewed by the force of the water. On shore, perhaps, this had not been apparent. The airmen could still hear the cheers across the harbour, but there was not much to cheer about. Moments into their flight they had lost the ability to steer the balloon. Now, for better or worse, it was the Arctic winds that would decide where they were carried.

For around half an hour the *Eagle* was still visible from the launch site. It was at 900 feet, or slightly lower, and swinging around to the east. It disappeared inside a cloud over the nearby Vogelsang Island and the men on Spitzbergen, at least, were never to see it again. Strindberg threw down the note for his lover as the balloon passed Vogelsang Island and moved out again across the open water. They were still inside the cloud, however, and without the sun to heat their balloon they were, once again, rapidly losing height. Soon the remaining third of their guidelines was slicing through the sea.

All was not lost, however. The men busied themselves splicing ballast lines to the ends of the guidelines, a job they finished at 4.24 pm, by which time the *Eagle* was at 1,600 feet and rising on a brisk west-southwest wind. Below them they could see the beginning of the pack ice and the sense of adventure quickened. They broke open bottles of ale. All was well and the team's boyishness burst through: Andrée climbed onto the connecting ring between the balloon and the gondola, stood to urinate, jokingly threatening to do so onto Fraenkel below.

Towards the end of the afternoon the blue sea darkened beneath them and soon the ice began in earnest. They had brought 36 carrier pigeons with them to send messages and now they despatched the first (which never arrived). They had their first dinner on board the *Eagle*, comprising sandwiches and broth with macaroni heated on a primus stove suspended some 26 feet below the gondola: Andrée wasn't risk-averse, but the proximity of fire and a balloon full of hydrogen was too much even for him. They ate their dinner, aware for the first time of the silence: a few birds shrieked and the balloon's valve was whistling, for some reason. Other than that, the only sound to be heard was the occasional collision or collapse among the ice floes beneath.

At 7.15 pm Andrée went below to sleep and the other two sat above, whispering together. The *Eagle* was now riding at about 2,200 feet above a layer of mist, which also extended to the north. To the south they could still make out the blue line of the sea. The two young men made more adolescent jokes about lightening the load by urinating over the side or spitting. What they did, in fact, at 9.43 pm was to throw overboard one of the marker buoys they had brought with them: they didn't want to risk sinking out of the sun.

At 11.10 pm Strindberg, scouring the horizon, noted a great bank of cloud in the east, towards which they seemed to be drifting. They were now at 1,600 feet. An hour later and they entered the cloud. Within four minutes there was ice on the guidelines and, without the sun, they had fallen dramatically; at times they went as low as 65 feet. Another 12 kilograms of ballast went overboard, but the cloud around them thickened so that all they could see was ice and water. By 1.26 am they were becalmed. When the wind picked up towards morning, it was not entirely good news: it was bearing them west. Now it was Andrée's turn to watch as his companions slept. He looked down outside and noted how easy it was to mistake areas of snow-free ice for clear water; he noticed, too, how varied the colours of the ice were. Here, now, beneath him, it was pale yellow.

Through the morning they picked up speed, ploughing on through light fog and drizzle, but at 3.06 pm the gondola crunched down onto the ice. The men raced to throw things overboard: out went another 25 kilograms of sand; out went the heavy knives they'd used to cut the ropes the previous day; and out too went the polar buoy. Clearly, this cannot have been a snap decision. They now realized that they would not make it to the Pole, whatever else their future held.

In the short term what it held was great discomfort. The Eagle was still weighed down by the freezing fog and the gondola crashed repeatedly into the ice. The three men endured several hours of this, being dragged across the hummocked floes, scraping, lifting, stamping back down, sometimes as often as every five minutes. Then it became every minute. By 10 pm they were not moving at all. Everything, even the balloon, was wet through.

Andrée waited up while the others slept, listening to the wind amid the icy guidelines and the ineffectual flapping of the sails. He wanted to marshal his thoughts. He was not a man whose public face hid troubled private waters. If he regretted his over-confidence about the Arctic weather, and his apparent failure to countenance the problem of fog and mist, he certainly didn't show it. Self-control was all and what he wrote in his diary was surely no different from what he rehearsed for his comrades: he was proud to have been the first to sail above the polar ice and, with that achievement and the mark on history that it brought, he was content to die, if that indeed was what lay ahead.

The Eagle, however, seemed to have other thoughts. It was straining to be off, twisting, tugging, rising, falling, almost willing the wind to grow stronger. Indeed, if they were airborne now, they would have been carried back to Spitzbergen. Then, as the wind picked up and it seemed certain that they would soon be off again, it shifted direction, away from safety. Eventually, the *Eagle* struggled skywards and it became apparent what had held them back: a guideline had fastened itself to a block of ice.

At midday, in the air at last, they sat down to dinner, cooked by Strindberg, as most of their food seems to have been from then on.[2] Fraenkel did the washing up. Below they could see polar-bear tracks out on the ice and the weather was discernibly colder. There was a thick hoarfrost on the rigging. At 1.08 pm they sent off another carrier pigeon. This one, almost miraculously, made it back to Stockholm. The message it carried was to be the last heard of Andrée's men by the outside world for quite some time.

Over the following 18 hours the balloon continued to scrape and jolt along the ice. The crushing blows were increasingly intolerable. Strindberg, for one, was beginning to feel seasick; rest was impossible. The fog was so thick they could see almost nothing. They threw increasing quantities over the side – another seven buoys, their winch, a box of medicines, 200 kilograms of provisions, 75 kilograms of sand – but any uplift was short-lived.

By the time the new day had come Andrée was eyeing up the ice-fields as best he could through the clouds, with a view to landing. Ironically, the balloon began to rise at about 5.28 am. By then they had, it seems, had enough. Within ten minutes they were letting out the valve and bringing the *Eagle*, finally, to rest. They made a text-book landing.

When raising finance for the expedition Andrée had said: 'The thing is so difficult that it is not worthwhile attempting it. The thing is so difficult that I cannot help but attempt it.' Yet the flight of the *Eagle* was nothing compared to the challenge that now faced the three men. It was 14 July. Shortly after 7.30 in the morning they set foot for the first time on the ice. The real adventure was about to begin.

---

2. They ate potage hotch-potch, chateaubriand, chocolate with biscuits, and more biscuits with raspberry syrup and water. They drank the King's Special Ale.

They now had a number of choices, none of them exactly good. They could stay where they were and drift with the ice, or, of course, they could walk. Their compatriot, the Norwegian national hero Fritjof Nansen, had spent the winter of 1895–6 on Franz Josef Land, and his survival there may well have inspired them. In any event, that was where they decided to direct their efforts. There was, after all, a large depot of stores there. The catch was, however, that Franz Josef Land was 210 miles away. They were nothing if not ambitious.

They also, it must be said, were not entirely sure where they were. As they couldn't see the sun or the stars, they couldn't take bearings. Nevertheless, they spent six days preparing themselves for what lay ahead. The three sledges that they had brought on the gondola were packed with provisions for six months, together with their scientific and photographic equipment, a canvas boat, a tent, a sleeping sack of deerskin, guns, and ammunition. Several times Andrée climbed onto the roof of the gondola to see if he could spy land, but he could not. Their environs were precarious, protean, untrustworthy: they were in a sea clogged with pack ice, where the spaces between the floes constantly closed and opened. The ice itself wasn't the flat, unvaried *tabula rasa* of the polar imagination; it was pitted and ridged and cracked. Down on the surface, just as from the balloon, it was easy to mistake pools of melted water for open sea.

Yet the three men were more than hopeful: they were optimistic. Their spirits were raised further when Andrée bagged a polar bear: the prospect of fresh meat, instead of the powdered substitute they had with them, was an entrancing one. Strindberg fried up some steaks and they all felt pleased with themselves.

They set off on the 22nd, each pulling a sledge with supplies weighing up to 440 pounds. It never stopped being hard, slow work. Over the next few days they worked out the best way to proceed: Andrée would scout ahead, clambering among the ice humps, testing out the twisting, deceptive pools of fresh water and mapping out the leads in his head. Beneath his feet fissures opened with no warning. Behind him Strindberg and Fraenkel stamped and shivered to keep off the cold.

Still, it was summer and the temperature hovered just above zero.

Once Andrée had made his decision, they tried to cut a path with spade and axe, but then discovered that getting the sledges over the hummocks was dangerous as well as slow. Often the sledges turned somersaults, slipping too quickly down the far side, spinning out of control. It was not as if they were easy things to manoeuvre, but they had to be moved through 90 degrees, sometimes in the middle of a tight pass. To vary the monotony the men sometimes switched to pulling one sledge at a time, the three of them together. When they had to cross the leads they unpacked the boat, loaded it up and ferried themselves across, trying not to think about what would happen if it capsized beneath the awkward weight of the sledges. Nevertheless, each of the sledges frequently slipped over the edge of the ice, the puller being dragged down and forced to lie still on the ice, a dead weight, until the others could rescue him. On the best of these days they could travel four miles.

They no longer bothered to observe the niceties of the clock. They slept when they needed to and pressed on whenever they could, whatever the time of day or night. They had not entirely abandoned routine, however. Each day began with Andrée greasing the team's boots, while Strindberg cooked polar-bear meat and Fraenkel attended to the tent and laid the table. They used a medicine chest, the crate with the photographic equipment and a chest containing their precious boxes of matches as seats. It was impossible to stay clean and they rarely washed, although it was Andrée's habit to grease his hands with polar-bear fat before they started, as he was keen to keep them soft.

Over the next few days progress was slow, though their camaraderie held. The 25th was Anna's birthday. The men celebrated it with cocoa and condensed milk, sandwiches and biscuits, and raised four hearty hurrahs to Strindberg's beloved. Chewing delightedly on a toffee, he wrote to her again, for the second time since they had grounded the *Eagle*. He believed that they were certain to reach home, and that his and Anna's future together would, of course, be bright and happy. The hardships were nothing as long as he could come home to her at last. Indeed, he and Fraenkel talked of home a great deal; Andrée was silent on the subject.

The following day they took stock. The sledges were unmanageable. The three agreed to trim the weight of each sledge down to around 300 lbs. Out, therefore, went a substantial quantity of provisions, but, rather than leave so much behind, the men found an excuse to indulge themselves. They gorged on biscuits and honey, and washed them down with the champagne that they had earmarked for the conquest of the Pole. They now took with them enough supplies for only another 45 days. As they got further south, they reasoned, they would be able to hunt more. As if to prove the point, that very day Strindberg bagged his first polar bear. They were gleeful: more fresh meat meant that they could ditch even more of the meat powder. They could also use the bearskin to mend their sleeping sack, which, with three men to cater for, was already under strain. Indeed, it was already quite unpopular: the reindeer hair seemed to get everywhere, even into the food.

Celebrations over, the next stage of their trek was exhausting. Waking at 5 pm, they kept on the go for 16 hours straight, despite a freezing wind from the north. The ice just now was smooth, as they'd hoped it all would be, and they crossed 14 leads. Even Fraenkel, by the end, was complaining of fatigue, but then his health seems to have been a greater cause for complaint than that of the others.

Andrée, meanwhile, seemed to be indefatigable. His observations of their surroundings were detailed and acute. He made precise notes about the strata in the ice and speculated about how they were formed; he collected odd specimens of plant life that he found caught in the ice; he gathered samples of the driftwood he found in the sea. When they shot an ivory gull to supplement the polar-bear meat, he squirreled away the gull's eyes, thinking that it would be interesting to study how the birds protected themselves from snow blindness. He noted, too, the call of the gull: 'pyot, pyot', modulating to 'piyrrr', a warning cry. He could even stand back from his own predicament to marvel at the beauty of the bleak environment. One morning he noted in his diary a 'magnificent Venetian landscape with canals between lofty hummock edges on both sides, a water square with ice fountain and stairs down to the canal. Divine.'

It was Strindberg who tracked their progress as best he could. His report on the 30th, the first time for some days that he could take his bearings, was not very reassuring. They needed to go southeast, but the ocean current was taking them due south. They resolved to tack east, but the next day the ice changed direction and took them west. The day after that they were carried back further north, despite an excellent day's progress. They simply could not walk fast enough to counter the drift of the ice they were walking upon.

On 3 August they stopped and regrouped. It was a fine day and the heat of the sun made the inside of the tent unbearable. All three of them took the opportunity to dry out their clothes. The clear weather meant that Strindberg could make more observations: over the previous four days they had drifted nearly eight miles to the north-northwest. The situation could not continue. They talked for a long time, but it was not until the next day that the decision was made to abandon the attempt to reach Franz Josef Land. There was another, smaller store to the southwest on Seven Islands, which they reckoned was six or seven weeks away. Thus far they had been on the ice for three.

They reviewed their food stocks and resolved to be more careful, but in the meantime they had just shot another polar bear, so they breakfasted, amid dense fog, on ribs, chops and kidneys, with a quarter-piece of bread each, and coffee and biscuits. They were becoming old hands: they knew which cuts of polar bear they preferred, that old polar-bear meat was better than new, and that it was better still if left in salt water for an hour or so. Each man carried his day's meat ration close to his body to keep it from freezing.

They were nothing if not resourceful, too – or at least Andrée and Strindberg were. At Andrée's instigation they tried eating the meat raw and found that it tasted rather like oysters. Andrée also showed Fraenkel how to make blood pancakes with oatmeal and butter. Strindberg concocted a kind of broth using algae from the edge of the ice floes, together with various powdered supplements from their supplies, and called it sea vegetable soup. Andrée professed to like it; the others were less sure.

By this point the shortcomings in their planning must have been apparent for some time. There was, as has been noted already, just one sleeping sack between the three of them, and, whether they shared it or took turns to use it, it was not conducive to rest. Then there were the clothes. Each of them had three or four changes of underclothes, an undershirt, a shirt, thin and thick drawers, and stockings. There were two woollen jerseys, four pairs of woollen mittens or gloves and a leather waistcoat. They each had a suit of rain-proof cloth, high boots, Lapp boots, puttees, a woollen cap, a fur cap and a cloth hood. This was not clothing for the Arctic: there was not enough leather or fur, and too much thin material cut for comfort and style, not survival. (Some of Strindberg's clothes were neatly monogrammed: perhaps they were gifts from his fiancée.)

The ice was becoming increasingly unpredictable. There was a lot of fresh water on the surface and new ice formed each night. Sometimes the men had to creep forward on all fours across the floes: the new ice was weak and potentially deadly. To make matters worse, on the 11th they discovered once again that, since they had changed direction, they had failed to maintain their course: they had gone 30 miles south-southwest, instead of southwest.

The temperature was now around -17.5° Fahrenheit. The winds were freezing and they all had catarrh streaming down their faces. Fraenkel was suffering from diarrhoea, which Andrée treated with opium. There were more animals to be seen now: gulls, seals, bears, a walrus. Less welcome, perhaps, were the fulmars, the carrion birds of the Arctic, which seemed to smell of rotten meat. On the same day that their supply of polar-bear meat ran out they spied a seal, but in their haste to bag it they missed their mark and it got away. Next they saw three polar bears, a mother and two cubs, but they remained resolutely distant. Andrée knew that they couldn't make the same mistake twice. He offered himself as bait, relying on his colleagues' marksmanship to keep him alive. They did not fail him this time and they now had enough meat for another 23 days.

Health was becoming a bigger problem. There were nagging injuries or ailments almost every day. Strindberg and Andrée both came down with diarrhoea, and Strindberg also got a bad cut on his hand and developed a boil on his upper lip. One day Fraenkel pulled so hard on his sledge that he dislocated his knee. Somehow Andrée pushed it back into place and Fraenkel carried on as before, even with cramp, diarrhoea, a cold and severe stomach pains. Andrée's response was to provide morphine and indulge in an unkind thought: 'We shall see if he can become a man again.' But then, when Fraenkel's foot failed him, it was Andrée who massaged it morning and evening, cleared the pus from a blister, washed the wound, and bandaged it. Soon, however, Fraenkel became too weak to pull his sledge. He could only help to push, as Andrée and Strindberg took turns to go back and retrieve it after they had made some halting progress with their own.

Every time Strindberg calculated their position, he found the same story: they were off course and, consequently, were still making excruciatingly slow progress. The ice and snow were now rock-hard, and there was ice inside the tent each morning as the men awoke. Andrée swept it clear two or more times a day, and found himself thinking more and more about home.

September brought the end of the polar summer. As if to mark the moment, they saw the sun catch the horizon at midnight and the whole world aflame. Briefly, faced with increasingly wide channels, they took to the water in their canvas boat. They made good progress, enjoying the splash of the oars in the glassy water and the cries of the gulls. When the ice closed around them once more they returned to the floes with renewed vigour. They celebrated Strindberg's birthday on the 4 September with extra food; Andrée had some letters for him from Anna and his family. Then, between the 6th and the 9th the drift ice carried them 18 miles northeast, the exact opposite direction to the one that they wanted. By the 12th they were stuck: the north-west wind was making it impossible for them to move. Worse, their supply of meat was close to being gone. 'Our position,' Andrée wrote in his diary, 'is not particularly good.' With heavy hearts they realized that they would have to winter on the ice.

Yet as soon as they had made what appeared to be a fateful decision, things began to improve. They identified a floe that they thought would last until the spring, Fraenkel's foot began to mend and Andrée devised a net with which they could fish. In three days they drifted some 45 miles south-southeast. Then, on 17 September, they spied land. It was White Island, at the easternmost edge of Svalbard. They called it New Iceland. It was glacial, and seemed brilliant and beautiful when the sun shone on it. Most of the land was beneath the ice, however, and it was by no means a suitable place to winter. Still, it was a sign of progress and the men felt elated.

The next day was the 25th anniversary of the accession of King Oscar II to the twin thrones of Sweden and Norway. Accordingly the three balloonists flew the union flag over their camp and prepared a banquet for themselves. The bill of fare was as follows:

— seal steak and ivory gull fried in butter and seal blubber, with seal liver, brain and kidneys, and bread and butter;
— chocolate with Mellin's food-flour, and Albert biscuits and butter;
— *gateau aux raisins*;
— raspberry syrup juice; and
— Antonio de Ferrara port of 1834, given to them by the king himself.

The meal was followed by a speech by Andrée, the singing of the national anthem, then yet more biscuits, with butter and cheese, and the drinking of one more glass of wine each.

As if energized by recent events, Strindberg began to build an ice hut in which they could winter on the floe. Between them they shot three seals, five gulls and a polar bear, stocking up so much food – enough to see them through until April – that they became seriously worried about the threat of predators: quite rightly, as it turned out, since they soon found polar bears foraging around their camp.

The temperature was dropping steadily. On the 28th they moved into their hut, taking their supplies of meat with them for safekeeping. The 29th and 30th were calm and uneventful, although the floe didn't seem to be making much if any headway past White Island. Dawn on 1 October seemed to promise a beautiful day, but at around 5.30 disaster struck. With a sound like thunder the ice beneath them disintegrated. The hut was intact, but it now hung over the edge, while their belongings were spread across several floes. The temperature continued to fall. As Strindberg wrote, when he next had the chance to, on the 3rd or the 4th, it was an 'exciting situation'.

Around this time Andrée filled up his diary and started making notes in a pocket notebook. Fraenkel stopped making meteorological observations on the 3rd. By the 5th they were on White Island, scouting for somewhere to camp. Despite rain and snow and ferocious winds, they managed to draw the sledges up onto the ice-free south-western shore and chose a spot around 600 feet higher for their base. Andrée and Fraenkel set about collecting driftwood; Strindberg got to work on another ice hut.

Nothing else is known of them. As far as the outside world was concerned they had vanished long before, when the last carrier pigeon was dispatched from the *Eagle* all those weeks earlier. Their fate remained an unsolved mystery until 1 September 1930, when two sealers, the *Isbjørn* and the *Bratvaag*, stopped off at White Island. Sailors from one of these ships found the sledges and then, climbing further, found two bodies in what remained of the tent, close by a rock wall. Neither was in the sleeping sack, or lying on bear skins. The stove was full of fuel. Andrée and Fraenkel, it seemed, had frozen to death together. Some 300 yards away to the north, in a crevice under a foot or so of rubble, lay the grave of Nils Strindberg. His feet still bore his monogrammed socks.

To Strindberg, in fact, belongs the very last communication from the crew of the *Eagle*. On Sunday 17 September, shortly after 7 am, he wrote a single word in his notebook: 'Home.'

The Zealot's Tale

*A goldsmith sets out on an attempt
to conquer Jerusalem*

Perhaps all adventurers are touched with madness. Of no one can this have been more literally true than of Thomas Tany, who surfaced in London during the Interregnum.

Tany was a goldsmith by trade and spent his early years at the sign of the Three Golden Lions in the Strand, close by Temple Bar. It seems plausible, if not likely, that exposure to the mercury then used in the smelting process loosened his grip on reality. In any event, he burst onto the already thriving radical religious scene on 23 November 1649, when it was revealed to him that he was 'a Jew of the tribe of Reuben' and that he must change his name from Thomas to Theaurau John. Five months later, on 25 April 1650, he proclaimed his intention of leading the return of his people, the Jews, to the Holy Land and of rebuilding the Temple of Solomon. It isn't clear whether he meant actual Jews – still officially excluded from England, as they had been since 1290 – or merely followers of his whom he designated Jews. Perhaps, though, the distinction is meaningless.

On 20 December 1650, Tany declared himself to be the Earl of Essex, a descendant of Henry VII and heir to the throne. Around the same time it was revealed to Tany that he was the High Priest of the Jews. A sometime fellow-traveller, Lodowick Muggleton, founder of his own radical sect, the Muggletonians, and no stranger to grandiose claims,[1] reported that Tany went so far as to circumcise himself. Tany, however, was on a roll. A brief spell in Newgate Prison the following year, for blasphemy, did nothing to dampen his fervour and the authorities, who seem to have been remarkably tolerant of him for some reason, soon released him.

Tany then removed himself to Eltham in Kent, where he busied himself making tents for his forthcoming expedition. On 8 June 1654 he was back in London, claiming the crown of France. He also kept up his claim to the crowns of England and Scotland, and variously claimed the crowns of Rome, Naples and Jerusalem into the bargain. On 30 December the same year a vision inspired him to approach Parliament armed with a long, rusty sword. He asked the doorman, a Mr Cooper, if he could deliver a petition and was told that he would have to find a member of Parliament who could deliver it on his behalf. An hour later Tany returned and attacked Cooper with his sword. He was quickly overpowered. His vision, it turned out, had inspired him to kill all the members of the House of Commons. Nevertheless, in another burst of magnanimity he was freed on bail before February 1655 was out.

Tany's next adventure involved sailing across the North Sea to

---

1. Muggleton claimed to be one of the four witnesses of the Apocalypse. The most extraordinary thing about Muggletonianism, however, is that the sect survived until the death of its last adherent in 1979.

the Netherlands to raise support for his long-planned liberation of the Holy Land. It doesn't appear to have been forthcoming, the Dutch clearly knowing an English idiot when they saw one. Tany, touchingly, decided to launch the invasion himself. He was not entirely alone, however: he had the assistance of one Captain James. It would be nice to able to record the date they launched their venture, the port they embarked at, the stores they took on board, the grand speeches at the quayside. Whatever else might be said about Tany, he was not a man to do anything without telling the world – loudly and at length – all about it. Language would have been no barrier, since even speaking in English, much of what he said was so obscure that fellow-speakers found him hard to follow.

Maybe, however, there was no dramatic leave-taking. Tany's craft was no more than a rowing boat, which hardly needs a quay to board from. No one knows how far Tany and James got, or what became of them. If they were picked up by a passing ship or fishing boat, it's hard to guess where a man who claimed to be Earl of Essex, King of the Jews and King of France might have been set down. It's always been assumed therefore, not unreasonably, that they drowned somewhere in the English Channel.

The Orientalists' Tales

*We explore some mysteries
of the medieval Orient*

Until Columbus wrenched Europe's attention irrevocably to the West, it was the East that exercised the collective imagination, and onto which endless fantasies of wealth and strangeness were projected. The East was where the sun first rose, and all things began and were closer, somehow, to the creation.

Carpini, for instance, reports that the Mongol hordes were defeated by a troglodyte people in the Caspian Mountains who

were not able to endure the terrible noise which, in that

place, the sun made at his uprising. For when the sun rose, they had to lay one ear upon the ground and to cover the other as best they could, lest they should hear that dreadful sound. They could not escape, for attempting to do so had destroyed many of them. Chingis Cham [that is, Genghis Khan] and his company therefore, seeing that they prevailed not, but continually lost some of their number, fled and departed out of that land. They took along with them a man and his wife, who lived the rest of their lives among the Tartars.[1] Being asked why the men of their country live under the ground, they said that at a certain time of year, when the sun rises, there is such an huge noise that the people cannot endure it. Moreover, they play upon cymbals, drums and other musical instruments to try to drown out the sound.

The East was also, of course, where the Earthly Paradise was believed to lie. Some authors were understandably vague about this. Pierre d'Ailly, the Cardinal of Cambrai,[2] for instance, in his *Imago Mundi* (1410), describes it as 'a very pleasant place situated in certain regions of the Orient, a long distance by land or sea from our habitable world'. Others, such as Giovanni dei Marignolli, were rather more precise:

from Seyllan[3] to Paradise, according to what the natives say

1. As was mentioned in a note to the Friar's Tale, it was customary in medieval Europe to conflate Tartars (or Tatars) with Mongols.
2. D'Ailly had a huge influence on Columbus and Columbus's copy of his works is still extant. It shows much underlining and many marginal notes – including the quotation above about Paradise – usually whenever d'Ailly confirms what Columbus wanted to believe: that the sea journey west from Spain to the Orient would be a short one. The statements favoured by Columbus include d'Ailly's confident assertions that 'it is evident that this sea is navigable in a very few days', and that 'between the end of Spain and the beginning of India is no great width'. It is interesting to speculate what Columbus might have done without such a reassuring if wholly inaccurate source of inspiration.
3. Ceylon, that is, Sri Lanka.

after the tradition of their fathers, is a distance of forty
Italian miles; so that, it is said, the sound of the waters falling
from the fountain of Paradise is heard there.

Marignolli's account of Paradise is probably a definitive one,
marrying a small degree of local knowledge with the accepted scholarly traditions of the West. 'Paradise is a place that really
exists upon the Earth,' he writes, confidently. It is, he notes, 'the
loftiest spot on the face of the Earth, reaching to the sphere of
the moon'. Remarkably, this sort of commonplace comment draws
forth from the usually unreliable d'Ailly has an uncharacteristic burst
of common sense, chiding the bewildered reader: 'You must not sup-
pose by this that it really reaches the circle of the moon, that is a
hyperbolic expression.'

Paradise is, Marignolli continues,

a place remote from all strife, delectable in balminess and
brightness of atmosphere, and in the midst whereof a
fountain springeth from the ground pouring forth its waters
to water, according to the season, the Paradise and all the
trees therein. And there grow all the trees that produce the
best of fruits; wondrous fair are they to look upon, fragrant
and delicious for the food of man. Now that fountain cometh
down from the mount and falleth into a lake, which is called
by the philosophers, Euphrates.

D'Ailly, by way of contrast and reverting to type, embellishes this
point with the common trope that 'the fall of these waters makes
such a noise that the people there are born deaf'.[4]

It was generally accepted that the four great rivers of the world
flowed out of Paradise:[5] the Gyon, which circled Ethiopia and

---

4. One wonders why both Paradise and the land where the sun rose – which both must
be considered places of hope – should have associations of extreme noise and
consequent loss of hearing.
5. They flowed back in at the North Pole. See the Clerk of Oxford's Tale.

became the Nile; the Phison,[6] which on Marignolli's account incorporated the Ganges, the Volga and the Yangtze; the Tigris;[7] and the Euphrates.

At different times Paradise was a city, a garden, a mountain, an island. Usually it was walled. Its principal location, however, was 'just beyond' the known world. As a consequence there are several stories about Alexander the Great and the Earthly Paradise. It was said, for instance, that when Alexander reached the end of his attempted conquest of the world, as he did in India, he set up a column to mark the limit of his achievement. In one version, having added India to his empire he reached a wide river that he believed was the Ganges. Taking some 500 men with him, he commandeered a nearby ship and sailed downstream. After a month's travel he and his army arrived at an immense city surrounded by a wall on all sides. A wandering Jew revealed to Alexander that the city accommodated the souls of the just as they waited for Judgement Day. In another story Paradise was a mountain, within a mile of which stood another peak of similar height. Alexander, lord of all the world, scaled the latter and demanded that Paradise pay him tribute. Its answer is unrecorded.

6. Marignolli is very forthcoming about the Phison: 'I believe it to be the biggest river of fresh water in the world, and I have crossed it myself. And it has on its banks very great and noble cities, rich above all in gold. And on that river excellent craftsmen have their dwelling, occupying wooden houses, especially weavers of silks and gold brocade, in such numbers – I can bear witness, having seen them – as in my opinion as do not exist in the whole of Italy. And they have on the shores of the river an abundance of silk, more indeed than all the rest of the world put together. And they go about on their floating houses with their whole families just as if they were on shore. This I have seen.'
7. Again, Marignolli is keen to add the authority of his own experience: 'It passes over against the land of the Assyrians, and comes down near Nineveh, that great city of three days' journey, to which Jonah was sent to preach and his sepulchre is there. I have been there also and stopped a fortnight in the adjoining towns which were built out of the ruins of the city. There are capital fruits there, especially pomegranates of wonderful size and sweetness, with all the other fruits that we have in Italy. And on the opposite side of the river is a city built out of the ruin of Nineveh, which is called Mosul.' This last statement, incidentally, is true.

The Grivy's Tale

*We attempt to recover the drowned lands
of East Anglia*

F or the most part the pleasurable unfamiliarity of old maps
derives from their errors. Sometimes, however, it is not
the fact that maps have changed that jolts the reader, it
is the fact that the world that the maps describe has changed.

A case in point is that of the Fens of northern Cambridgeshire
and surrounding counties. The Mercator-Hondius Atlas, for instance,
contains a map of the area together with a description of what it calls
'the drowned lands': it's disorienting to see the familiar coastline broken and a large tract of land, perhaps 40 miles from east
to west, under water from south of the Wash to Ely and beyond.

It was not all submerged, however. There was a network of islets and islands trapped by six flooding rivers, among them the Nene and the Ouse. In summer the ditches and channels might be lush and green, but in winter the area became ocean, with water stretching to the horizon. The local population harvested the thick summer grass and hay, which they called *lid*, and in the autumn burned off the rest as stubble, presenting unwary travellers with the unnerving sight of smoke and flames rising strangely out of the dark November waters.

The locals had little time for travellers or for any other people from the outside, whom they called uplanders, 'being rude, uncivil and envious' to them, says Camden in his *Britannia* (1586).[1] They themselves were called 'Grivy' in Saxon times and latterly Fen-men or Fen-dwellers, and they stalked between islands on high stilts.

They could afford to be rude, since they wanted for nothing. There were six inland fisheries listed in the *Domesday Book*, among them Wisbech, and William of Malmesbury, writing at the end of the 12th century, noted that 'So great store there is of fishes that strangers coming hither make a wonder at it, and the inhabitants laugh thereat to see them wonder.' On summer nights, he continued, when the eels run, and especially if there is thunder in the air, the Fen-men would take to their channels and drains with their nets, and fill three or four barrels with dark writhing eels. Besides these there were pike, perches and roaches in great number, and the pools and lakes were crowded with coots and ducks, and other water birds, so many, says William, that two or three thousand could be netted when they were moulting and unable to fly.

The river banks and islets were rich with reeds and sedge, in which the wind was always whispering, and the islands themselves were home to alders, willows and other water-loving trees, all of which meant timber and thatch, and fuel for the fire. Many trees were also planted to help to bind the river banks more strongly and slow the tidal currents. Some of the larger islands, such as the Isle of Ely and Thorney Island, were thriving. William of Malmesbury compared the latter to 'a very Paradise, a heaven for the delight and

1. Perhaps this is the reason why Leyland, in his *Itinerary* of 1536, in which he traversed the length and breadth of the country, contrived to omit entirely the Fens and all points further east.

beauty thereof'. Its green fields were perfectly level and true, while the trees were so tall that they strived to reach the stars. Small hillocks bore apple trees and orchards, and the fields were full of vines, some on the ground, some raised up on poles.

Most of the watercourses twisted their black way through the islets and, some said, yielded 'a duskish vapour' that was not altogether savoury. The complex, slightly alien landscape was one reason why Hereward the Wake could successfully hide in the Fens while he led the Saxon resistance to the Norman Conquest. It is said he built himself a wooden castle and hid among the mists; certainly the Normans never found him. 'The natural strength of this place and plenty of all things here,' notes Camden cautiously, 'seditious rebels have often presumed.'

The Fens weren't successfully drained until after the English Civil Wars, although there had been plenty of schemes before, usually in the hands of monopolists such as Sir Robert Carr, whom James I appointed in return for a percentage of the spoils. Ben Jonson ridiculed the attendant greed and vanity in *The Devil is an Ass* (1616), in which one Fabian Fitzdottrel of Norfolk is tricked into believing that he will become the Duke of Drown'd Land. 'All Crowland / Is ours,' he tells his wife,

And the Fens, from us in Norfolk
To the utmost bounds of Lincolnshire! We have view'd it,
And measur'd it within all, by the scale:
The richest tract of land, love, in the kingdom!
There will be made seventeen or eighteen millions,
Or more, as't may be handled! Wherefore think,
Sweetheart, if thou hast a fancy to one place
More than another, to be duchess of,
Now name it.

If there is an echo here of the tale of the painter's wife, the story of whom opens the Courtier's Tale, perhaps that is no accident. Jonson knew Raleigh well and he certainly knew Raleigh's *History of the World*, published a couple of years previously. Indeed, Jonson characteristically, claimed to have written some of it.

The
Dancer's
Tale

*Some adventurers make fools of themselves
in the name of exploration*

ales of the European exploration of the Americas, especially where they touch on dealings with the luckless inhabitants they encountered, reveal many qualities: resilience, cruelty, dishonesty, camaraderie, barbarism and a dozen more besides. One that no one in their right mind would usually apply to them is, arguably, charm, except perhaps in one instance.

Sir John Davis was one of many who followed in Frobisher's wake and went in search of the Northwest Passage. In 1585 Davis reached the coast of North America with two ships, the *Sunshine* and the *Moonshine*. Approaching the shore, they anchored, and their crews went on land to look for fresh water and firewood. They soon found signs of human habitation: some leatherwork, a piece of fur, a small shoe. They climbed a high rock to look about. Almost immediately they were spotted by the natives, who, in Davis's words, 'made a lamentable noise, as we thought, with great outcries and screechings'. Davis initially mistook their cries for the howling of wolves. 'At last I halloed again,' says Davis, 'and they likewise cried.'

Finally the Englishmen saw the natives: some were on the shore, others in a canoe rowing towards an island close by. Davis and his small company on shore raised a great shout, 'partly to allure them to us,' he wrote, 'and partly to warn our company of them'. The story could easily have gone the way of many other such encounters, with the Europeans' suspicion and fear winning out. ('The people in these parts are all treacherous,' Luke Fox told his men when going ashore, 'howsoever fair they treat you.')

No doubt there were contingency plans for such occasions. Certainly it's hard to see why else the men back on board would have been inspired by the ship's musicians to rescue their captain. One imagines that subsequent relations between captain and officers would be somewhat strained otherwise. But that is what they did, 'purposing either by force to rescue us, if need so require,' says Davis, 'or with courtesy to allure the people'.

When the musicians made land they played their instruments, and Davis and his men danced, 'making,' he says, 'many signs of friendship'. It must have been a peculiar sight, to say the least: a small group of Englishmen dancing – who knows what? perhaps a jig or a simple country circle dance learned in childhood – on a bleak and distant shore, watched by an audience to whom both the music and the dance were wholly and irrevocably alien, and might just as well have been beamed down from Mars for all the sense they made. The sailors, too, must have asked themselves, somewhat disbelievingly, if they had really braved a journey to the ends of the Earth in order to caper like drunkards on the sands.

Whatever the natives thought of it, however, they were understandably intrigued. Ten canoes came into view from nearby islands. Two came close enough to shore to talk to Davis. Neither party understood a word the other said, but Davis persisted in alluring them with 'friendly embracings and signs of courtesy'. At length one of the natives pointed to the sun and then struck himself on the breast 'so hard,' said Davis, 'that we might hear the blow'. This he did repeatedly. John Ellis, the master of the *Moonshine*, was then given the unenviable task of working out how to gain the native's friendship. Ellis copied him, striking his breast and pointing to the sun. Somehow this broke the ice. The natives came on shore, and the Englishmen threw them their caps, stockings and gloves, and 'such other things as then we had about us, playing with our music and making signs of joys and dancing'. So they continued until the night fell and the Englishmen returned to their ships, bidding their new friends farewell.

The
Legate's
Tale

A self-important papal legate pays court
to the Queen of Sheba

G iovanni dei Marignolli was a Florentine, born in the latter part of the 13th century. He became a Franciscan and in 1338 was chosen by Pope Benedict XI to become one of four papal legates to the court of the Great Khan at Cambaleth (now Beijing). It was not, on the face of it, an enviable assignment. The Pope wished the legates to convey letters and presents to an emperor who, in Marignolli's words,

> holds the sway of nearly half the eastern world, and whose
> power and wealth, with the multitude of cities and provinces

and languages under him, and the countless number, as I may say, of the nations over which he rules, pass all telling.

It is hard not to imagine that the Khan and his empire made Europe's assorted rulers and potentates feel rather insignificant. Certainly this was no imperious mission to benighted savages: there was a proper and appropriate respect for Mongol achievements and, of course, for Mongol power.

As a source, then, Marignolli ought really to be unimpeachable. Integrity and honesty, one might think, were requisite qualities for the role of diplomat. Yet we have the story of his travels only because, on his return, he was commanded by the Emperor Charles IV to redraft the Annals of Bohemia. So unexciting did he find this exercise that he amused himself by interpolating his recollections of the road to the Mongol court and beyond. If he was tempted to embellish in such a context, his thoughts turning wistfully, perhaps, towards the griffins prowling the margins of medieval bestiaries, then he could hardly be blamed in such a dry and barren environment.

In any event, Marignolli's narrative begins with admirable qualities, such as clarity and accuracy, that are not always evident in medieval writings on any subject, never mind barbarian geography. Marignolli left Avignon, where the Papacy then resided, in December 1338. He was in Naples by Lent in 1339, waiting there for a Genoese ship that was bringing envoys from the Khan to the Pope with a request for an alliance. By 1 May they had arrived at Constantinople; they then stayed at Pera, a little along the coast, for the best part of two months. They were still there on 24 June for the feast of St John the Baptist. Soon afterwards they crossed the Black Sea, a journey of eight days, to Caffa, a thriving Genoese port on the coast of Crimea, which could boast as many as 200 masts in its harbour on any given day. (It is known now, 600 years or more after its zenith, as Feodosiya, in southern Ukraine.)

From Caffa the diplomats made their way to the court of Öz Beg, leader of the legendary Golden Horde and ruler of the western arm of the Mongol empire, at Sarai on the upper Volga (as noted in the Merchant's Tale, this was somewhere near modern Volgograd). There they wintered before continuing to Armalec (now Kuldja in western China).

Armalec, as Marignolli describes it, was the capital of the middle region of the Mongol empire. Marignolli and his fellow legates bought a piece of ground, built a church, dug wells and gave every impression of hunkering down for the long term. They sang masses, and preached freely and openly. This, it must be said, took some courage: only the previous year, Marignolli reports, the bishop and six other friars in the city had, in his words, 'undergone a glorious martyrdom'.

If the Pope had been keen to come to terms with the Great Khan as rapidly as possible, he clearly failed to impress the point on Marignolli and his companions, since it was at least two years before the party moved on from Armalec. Eventually, however, they evidently felt that they should make the effort to complete their assignment. Before them lay the salt lakes of the Hangayn Mountains, and the rocks and sand of the northern reaches of the Gobi. It was territory that, as Marignolli observes rather smugly, used to be thought impassable prior to the arrival of the Mongol hordes. 'Pass it, however, the Tartars did,' he notes. 'And so did I. Twice.'

From there the legates and their retainers came to Cambaleth, where the Khan entertained them royally for a further three years. They lived, all 32 of them, in imperial apartments, being waited on by two Mongol princes:

> This they did in the most liberal manner, not merely as
> regards meat and drink, but even down to such things as
> paper for lanterns, while all necessary servants were also
> detached from the court to wait upon us… And I should
> add that they kept us and all our establishment clothed in
> costly raiment.

Marignolli, who was not so unworldly as all that, went so far as to calculate how much the Khan had spent and found the large sum of money that emerged at the end of his calculations rather pleasing. True, he does have a stab at suggesting that he was above all such things – 'nothing would induce me to abide there,' he wrote, once they had decided to leave – but it rings a little hollow after nearly four years in which, as far as one can tell, he abode quite happily with nary a squeak of discontent.

In any event, Marignolli says with some satisfaction, on their departure the Khan, having begged them to stay, pressed on them three year's expenses and the recommendation that Marignolli should be returned speedily to Cambaleth by the Pope, this time with the rank of cardinal. With what modesty Marignolli rebuffed the compliment we can only imagine. The Khan made only one stipulation when they left, and that was that they should travel home via India, because the road across Eurasia was closed because of war. It is here that Marignolli's narrative begins to get really interesting.

The legates first journeyed south to 'that most famous city of Campsay', known today as Hang-Chou, near the mouth of the Ch'ien-t'ang River. It was a city at its peak, the greatest commercial centre in the whole Mongol empire.[1] Marignolli, like Marco Polo before him, adored it. It was, he wrote,

> the finest, biggest, richest, the most populous and altogether
> the most marvellous city, the city of the greatest wealth and
> luxury, of the most splendid buildings, especially idol temples,
> in some of which there are 1,000 and 2,000 monks dwelling
> together, that exists now on the face of the Earth or mayhap
> that ever did exist.

It's not difficult to sense him getting carried away with the thought of the place just writing about it: 'When authors tell of its ten thousand noble bridges of stone,[2] adorned with sculptures and statues of armed princes, it passes the belief of one who has not been

1. It would soon go into decline, eclipsed by other ports and cities, most recently Shanghai. Its population today is no larger, and possibly less, than it was when Marignolli visited.
2. To be fair, this is slightly less ridiculous than the 12,000 bridges ascribed to it in the Mercator-Hondius Atlas, some of them so big that ships might, the text claims, pass under them with their masts upright and under full sail.

there. And yet these authors do not lie.'

From Campsay Marignolli passed further south, to Zayton,[3] then the principal Chinese port. Its significance to global trade can be measured by the fact that some 100,000 Arab traders are said to have lived there. Today it is Ch'uan-chou, in the province of Fukien. From there Marignolli sailed on St Stephen's (Boxing) Day 1347, to Columbum (Quilon in Kerala, southwestern India), arriving at Easter 1348. Then his travels began to get somewhat confused.

What Marignolli *says* is that, shortly after arriving in Columbum, he decided to visit the shrine of St Thomas in Madras, on the eastern coast of India. On the journey they

> encountered so many storms commencing from St George's
> Eve and were so dashed about by them, that sixty times and
> more we were all but swamped in the depths of the sea, and
> it was only by divine miracle that we escaped. And such
> wondrous things we beheld! The sea as if in flames, and fire-
> spitting dragons flying by. As they passed they slew persons
> on board the other junks, while ours remained untouched by
> God's grace…

From Madras he seems to have returned to Columbum and stayed there for some 16 months, preaching, baptizing converts and – it must be said – enriching himself. For reasons that will become apparent, he breaks off his narrative for an outburst about the pepper trade:

> Now this pepper grows on a kind of vine, which are planted
> just like in our vineyards. These vines produce clusters which
> at first are like those of the wild vine, of a green colour, and
> afterwards are almost like bunches of grapes, and they have a
> red wine in them which I have squeezed out on my plate as a
> condiment. When they have ripened they are left to dry
> upon the tree, and when shrivelled by the excessive heat the
> dry clusters are knocked off with a stick and caught upon

3. According to some historians, this is probably where the word 'satin' comes from.

linen cloths, and so the harvest is gathered.

So far, so good – but, clearly, Marignolli had some obscure score to settle:

> These are things that I have seen with my eyes and handled
> with my hands during the 14 months I stayed there. And
> there is no roasting of the pepper, as authors have falsely
> asserted, nor does it grow in forests, but in regular gardens;
> nor are the Saracens [by which Marignolli means the non-
> Christian Indians] the proprietors, but the Christians of St
> Thomas. And these latter are the masters of the public
> steelyard, from which I derived, as a perquisite of my office as
> Pope's legate, every month a hundred gold fan, and a
> thousand when I left.[4]

As we have seen, Marignolli was not an overly humble man, but now he is quite clearly boasting:

> After I had been there some time, I went beyond the glory of
> Alexander the Great when he set up his column. For I
> erected a stone as my landmark and memorial in the corner

4. If anyone finds Marignolli's pecuniary interests here a little mercenary for an ambassador of God's regent on Earth, he does at least provide an apostolic precedent. Recalling the fact that the Apostle Thomas, like his master, was a carpenter, Marignolli tells that Thomas, in building his church, cut down a vast tree on Adam's Mount in Seyllan (that is, Sri Lanka) and brought it down to the sea using nothing but his girdle. Here he commanded the log to float itself to a particular beach on the mainland, which it did. The king of that region wished to raise it from the water, but fully ten thousand of his finest soldiers were unable to complete the task. Thomas then arrived on an ass, wearing, somewhat gaudily for a saint one feels, a shirt, a stole and a mantle of peacock feathers, with two great lions by his side. Naturally, he did the trick with the girdle again and the king, as seems to have been customary on such occasions, was converted to Christianity. Somewhat less conventionally, says Marignolli, the king also granted Thomas – clearly a more practical man than many of his saintly peers –'a perpetual [monopoly] of the public steelyard for pepper and all aromatic spices, and no one dares take this privilege from the Christians but at the peril of death'.

of the world over against paradise, and anointed it with oil. In sooth it was a marble pillar with a stone cross upon it, intended to last until the world's end. And it had the Pope's arms and my own engraved upon it, with inscriptions both in Latin and Indian characters. I consecrated and blessed it in the presence of an infinite multitude of people, and I was carried on the shoulders of the chiefs in a litter or palanquin like Solomon's.[5]

Alexander the Great *and* Solomon: is our legate getting delusions of grandeur? Let's see what he does next: 'After accomplishing many glorious works I went to see the famous Queen of Saba.'[6] Now, to the extent that he actually *did* visit a Queen of Sheba, the consensus is that he is talking about Java. He clearly isn't talking about the real Saba/Sheba, which was in southwestern Arabia, somewhere in the vicinity of modern Yemen. Why he would have sailed from south-western India back east to the foot of the Malay Peninsula (which Ptolemy, wonderfully, called the Golden Chersonese) is anyone's guess. In any event, Marignolli's Saba was an island in a mildly Amazonian tradition:

in that island women always, or for the most part, have held the government in preference to the men. And in the palace there I have seen historical pictures representing women seated on the throne with men on bended knees adoring before them. And so also I saw that actually in that country the women sat in the chariots or on the elephant chairs, while the men drove the oxen or the elephants.

5. This column was seen on the shore as late as 1662 by a Dutch chaplain whose name has been lost, but it seems to have been washed away some time during the 19th century.
6. Perhaps it was the mention of Solomon that nudged Marignolli along here. Bilqis, the biblical Queen of Sheba, visited the court of Solomon to test his legendary wisdom. The obvious challenge to Marignolli's story – that for him to have met her she must have been, very roughly, 2,300 years old – doesn't seem to have bothered him.

Getting the bit between his teeth in describing the strangeness of the place, Marignolli later adds that

> there the sun rises just the opposite of here and at noon the
> shadow of a man passes from left to right, instead of from
> right to left, as it does here. The North Pole there was six
> degrees below the horizon and the South Pole as much
> elevated above it…

Just for good measure, he assures his readers that the prophet Elijah could still be seen sometimes walking its hills.

To be fair to the man, Marignolli may at this point have been experiencing delusions as a result of extreme bad health. It's rare in this kind of text for people to write much about illness and bodily (mis)functions; reading Marignolli, you can see why. 'I was passing pieces of flesh from my intestines with a vast amount of blood, and suffered from an incurable dysentery for something like eleven months,' he tells us at one point, with a patient's grim pleasure at recounting his symptoms. It was, of course, life-threatening – 'a disease such as they say no one ever escaped from with life' – yet he recovered. This was solely down to 'a certain female physician of the Queen's', who clearly had yet to encounter contemporary western medical theory, with its fatal fascination for bloodletting, a fact for which Marignolli should have been extremely grateful. Instead, she cured him 'simply by certain juices of herbs and an abstinent diet'.[7]

Naturally, this being Marignolli, the Queen soon recognized his qualities. According to his account:

> I frequently saw the Queen and gave her my benediction. I
> rode upon her elephant and was present at a magnificent
> banquet of hers. And while I was seated on a chair of state in
> the presence of the whole city she honoured me with splendid

7. Marignolli, ever alert where wealth is at stake, is clear about the cause of his misery. It is 'the result of a very powerful poison I had swallowed in Columbum, administered by those who wished to plunder my property'.

presents. For she bestowed on me a golden girdle, such as she was accustomed to confer upon those whom she had created princes or chiefs... She also bestowed raiment on me, that is to say, 150 whole pieces of very delicate and costly stuff. Of these I took nine for our lord the Pope, five for myself, gave three apiece to each of the chief among my companions, with two apiece to the subordinates, and all the rest I distributed in the Queen's own presence among her servants who stood around, so that they might perceive that I was not greedy.

Finally bidding farewell to the Queen, Marignolli sailed back west to 'Seyllan' – Ceylon, now Sri Lanka – which is 'over against Paradise'. It's an island with a long and venerable tradition of errors attached to it. Marco Polo, demonstrating where he got his reputation for exaggeration from, claimed that it had a circumference of 2,400 miles – and that in ancient times that had been 3,600 miles, according to some unspecified maps that Polo has seen. (The correct figure is more like 700 miles.) When it comes to errors, however, Polo was a mere amateur compared to the third-century Roman geographical writer Julius Solinus, known as *Polyhistor*, teller of varied tales.[8]

8. Solinus wasn't an original thinker or researcher. He redacted the information in his *Collectanea rerum memorabilium* from a range of earlier sources. His particular skill, however, in the words of one modern historian, was to 'extract the dross and leave the gold'. Given that everyone from St Augustine of Hippo down to Columbus drew on his work, the same historian states that it is 'doubtful if anyone else over so long a period has ever influenced geography so profoundly or so mischievously'. Still, it is hard not to warm to a Roman writer on geography who can confidently open his work with the statement that Italy is 1,400 miles long and shaped like an oak leaf, broader than it is long; or casually throw out the observation that tigers are 'notable for the goodly spots wherewith their coats are powdered'. Open his work anywhere and it is a challenge to find something that might be true. He makes Mandeville – who undoubtedly took some of his prodigies and freaks of nature from Solinus's pages – seem like an overcautious stickler for accuracy. Sadly, Solinus's book has been translated into English only once – in 1587, by Arthur Golding, author of Shakespeare's favourite translations of Ovid. Indeed, it would be nice to think that Shakespeare learned his cavalier disregard for the niceties of cartographical accuracy from the master: certainly one feels Solinus would have instinctively warmed to a writer capable of giving Bohemia a coast, or making Milan a seaport.

Mathew Lyons

Calling the island by another of its several names, Taprobane, Solinus notes that the greater part of the island is 'waste wilderness', being 'parched with heat'.[9] Oddly for Solinus, the population has the usual number of limbs for humans, all of which are in the usual proportion; however, they do live to at least 100. Among other pastimes, they spend their days ransacking the sea for sea tortoises, the shells of which are so huge that 'one of them will make a house able to receive a household of many persons without pestering'.

Marignolli's interest in 'Seyllan' was biblical. As already noted, it was believed to be close to the Earthly Paradise. At its centre was an 'exceeding high mountain [with] a pinnacle of surpassing height, which, on account of the clouds, can rarely be seen'. When Adam was cast out of Paradise,

> the angel took [him] by the arm and set him down beyond
> the lake on the mountain of Seyllan… And by chance Adam
> planted his right foot upon a stone and, by a divine miracle,
> the form of the soles of his foot was imprinted on the marble.
> There it is to this very day. And the size thereof is two and a
> half of our palms.

Close by this on the mountainside, 'still at a great height', is

> the house of Adam, which he made with his own hands. It is
> of an oblong quadrangular shape like a sepulchre, with a door
> in the middle, and is formed of great tabular slabs of marble,
> not cemented, but merely laid one upon the other. It is said
> by the natives that the deluge never mounted to that point
> and thus the house has never been disturbed.

Just to round things off, Marignolli notes that the city of Kotte was founded by Cain after he had slain Abel. Perhaps betrayal was on Marignolli's mind:

9. Taprobane is an anomaly, a real place with quasi-mythical status. Tommaso Campanella located his Utopia there in his radical text *The City of the Sun* (1602).

Here a certain tyrant by name Coya Jaan… at first putting on a pretence of treating us honourably, by and by in the politest manner and under the name of a loan, took from us 60,000 marks, in gold, silver, silk, cloth of gold, precious stones, pearls, camphor, musk, myrrh and aromatic spices, gifts from the Great Khan and other princes to us, or presents sent from them to the Pope. And so we were detained, with all politeness, by this man, for four months.

It must have been galling indeed.

It was certainly the end of Marignolli's wanderings. From Sri Lanka he slowly made his way back to Europe by way of Hormuz, Mesopotamia and Jerusalem, arriving at the papal court in Avignon in 1353. After the grand bilking he had received in Sri Lanka he had little to show for all his efforts. All that we know he had with him was an umbrella, something of a novelty. So rare was it, in fact, that it had yet to be given a name in any European language: it was simply a nameless 'thing like a little tent-roof on a cane handle, which [the natives] open out at will as a protection against sun and rain'. Marignolli paraded with it around Florence, proud to the last.[10]

---

10. Despite much of the foregoing, Marignolli was something of a rationalist. He didn't believe in races of monstrous people, for instance, and thought that the existence of umbrellas explained the myth of the monoscelans, who appear in both Solinus's and Mandeville's texts, to name but two, and who are 'people such as have been invented who have but one foot which they use to shade themselves withal'. Elsewhere Marignolli notes drily, regarding God's command that the serpent be condemned to crawl on its belly, that 'I must say that I have seen many serpents, and very big ones too, that went with half the body quite erect, like women when they walk in the street, and very graceful to look upon.'

The Spanish Admiral's Tale

*A rediscovered narrative seems to prove the
existence of the Northwest Passage*

T he 18th century saw a renewal of interest in the
Northwest Passage, after a considerable period of
indifference. This was due in no small measure to the
discovery and publication of a letter from Bartolomeo de Fonte,
sometime Admiral of New Spain and Peru, and latterly Prince of
Chile. The letter itself appears to be undated, but it refers to a journey of 1640 in search of the longed-for straits from the west, an
approach that the English, at least, were ill-equipped to make, given
Spanish hegemony over the western Americas at that point. It was
first published in the *Monthly Miscellany, or Memoirs for the Curious* in

two issues, those of April and June 1708.

According to Fonte, the impetus behind his exploration was a direct command from the royal court of Spain, which had watched the progress, if it can be called that, of the English with interest. (As we know, the Spanish had a well-placed spy aboard for Frobisher's third voyage and it's not unlikely they had others.) Fonte therefore fitted out four ships – the *St Spiritus*, the *St Lucia*, the *Rosario* and the *King Philip* – and set out to the north from Callao in Peru on 3 April 1640.

Four days and two hundred leagues later they were in the Bay of Guajaquil (Guayaquil, in modern Ecuador), anchored in the port of St Helena. There, Fonte reports – perhaps rather surprisingly to a modern sensibility – everyone drank 'a quantity of bitumen of a dark colour with a cast of green, an excellent remedy against the scurvy and dropsy'. Perhaps, though, Fonte expected his letter's unknown recipient to look askance at this, too: he swiftly adds that bitumen 'is used as tar for shipping, but we took it in for medicine. It boils out of the earth, and is there in plenty.' Then again, bitumen was considered a palliative against an array of conditions in ancient times, so perhaps this was just another tradition dying hard. In any event, there is certainly no mention in Fonte's report of any ill-effects.

By 10 April Fonte and his men were crossing the equator and by the 11th they were anchored in the mouth of the St Jago River, where Fonte was impressed by the 'abundance of good fish', the no less abundant goats and wild pigs, not to mention the turkey cocks – of which his men bought 240 – the hens and ducks, and the quantities of excellent fruit.

By the end of the month, probably, they were anchored off the coast of what is now the State of Colima in western central Mexico. There they picked up a master mariner and six other seamen, all of whom had experience of trading for pearls with the natives off the eastern coast of Baja California. They also picked up an interesting bit of information: the master mariner told Fonte that California was an island. The oceans, he said, met again 200 leagues north of Cape St Lucas, the southernmost tip of Baja

Mathew Lyons

California.[1] Fonte despatched Don Diego Pennelossa, 'a young nobleman of great knowledge and address in cosmography and navigation', up what is now called the Gulf of California to find out the truth of the matter. Fonte himself then sailed on up the west coast.

Some 160 leagues further north-northwest, on 22 June, they reached an archipelago, which Fonte named after St Lazarus. From there they bore eastwards, up a quiet river into a large lake full of islands. The people, like the weather, were friendly and unthreatening. Fonte named the lake Lake Valasco, and noted how plentiful were the salmon trout and how large the white perch, some of which exceeded two feet in length. Then Fonte split his ships again, sending one Captain Barnada off to the north-northeast, towards the Pole and the 'Tartarian Sea' that was thought to surround it. Fonte himself sailed northeast up the Riolos Reyes River to a Native American town called Conosset, on the south side of Lake Belle. It was, he thought, a pleasant place. He stopped to admire the salmon, salmon

1. Fonte seems to have been more excited than surprised by this. It is true that when the Spanish first discovered California, in the 1530s, they had believed it to be an island and had named it after one mentioned in the hugely popular 14th-century Spanish chivalric romance, *Amadís of Gaul*. It's arguably the only example of a real place being named after a fictional one. The version of Amadís by Garcia Ordóñez de Montalvo, known as the *Exploits of Esplandian* (1508), relates that 'on the right hand of the Indies, very near to the Terrestrial Paradise, there is an island called California, which is peopled with black women, without any men among them, for they were accustomed to live in the fashion of Amazons'. (Sometimes one wonders if explorers ever thought it possible for an undiscovered island to be inhabited by anyone else.) If it occurred to the Spanish that the Earthly Paradise, insofar as it actually existed, was usually located near Ceylon (aka Taprobane, aka Sri Lanka) – that is, some 9,000 miles away – they appear not to have seen any problem with the discrepancy. Chivalric romances notwithstanding, it's equally true that in some quarters debate still flourished in the 17th century regarding the true geography of California, not least among the lesser cartographers. Indeed, as late as 1709 one Herman Moll wrote that 'it was long dubious whether [California] be a peninsula or an island, but at last the Spaniards sailed quite round'. However, one might have expected someone as senior in the Spanish colonial administration as Fonte to know that Francisco de Ulloa, under the patronage of Hernán Cortés, had realised that Baja California was a peninsula as long ago as 1539, a full 100 years earlier. Still, perhaps Chile was something of a backwater. On the other hand, we shouldn't judge the man too harshly. Mercator's map of 1595 contrives to place California within the Arctic Circle.

trout, pikes, perch and mullets abounding in both the river and the lake. The mullets in particular, he thought, were the most delicately flavoured in the world.

On the 27th he heard from Barnada, who strikes a similarly culinary note. Aside from the bread, salt, oil and brandy already on board, Barnada had been delighted to discover three kinds of venison in the country they sailed through, together with, as we might expect, excellent fish.

In any event, Fonte continued out of Lake Belle along a river that he named Parmentiers, after the expedition's interpreter. After six days they discovered another vast lake, some 600 miles long. Perhaps, like Raleigh before him[2], Fonte had grown soft on high living; once again it seems to have been the next meal that drew most of his attention. The lake itself was full of 'very large and well-fed' cod and ling; its islands and shores were home to moose that grew fat in winter eating the rampant moss; to wild cherries, strawberries, hurtleberries and wild currants; to wild fowl, heath cocks and hens, partridges, turkeys, and gulls.

By now, having dragged his attention away from the dinner table, Fonte had noticed a severe deterioration in the weather as they headed east. On 17 July Fonte's interpreter heard that the expedition would soon encounter another ship like theirs: it turned out to be sailing from Boston (then a small colonial town less than ten years old) under a Captain Shipley.

Fonte invited Shipley and his men aboard his own ship on the 30th, and pressed a diamond ring – worth, he said, 1,200 pieces of eight – on the overwhelmed English skipper. 'The modest gentleman received [it] with difficulty,' Fonte noted; he promptly offered Shipley another 1,000 pieces of eight for his charts and journals.

At this point, inexplicably, Fonte turned around for the journey home, apparently believing that there was no Northwest Passage to be found. This seems very odd, since the evidence of the Boston ship – to say the least – tends the other way. (Benjamin Franklin thought so, since he once sent a friend a 14-page letter detailing his arguments as to why Fonte's letter proved the existence of the Northwest Passage.)

2. See the Courtier's Tale.

Mathew Lyons

Fonte shortly received a letter from Barnada confirming that mountains and ice had blocked any potential passage through to Davis's Strait. For all he knew, Barnada wrote, somewhat sententiously, it had been like that since the creation, 'for mankind knew little of the wonderful works of God, especially near the north and south poles'.

Fonte's letter didn't make a huge splash on its first appearance in English, but it did when it was picked up and published in a book called *The Great Probability of a North West Passage*, in 1748. The book is credited to its mapmaker, Thomas Jefferys, the royal cartographer, though its text was probably the work of a little known man named either Charles Swain or Theodore Swain Drage.

As for Fonte, he remains a special case. It's not just that the journey he describes could never have been made: he himself never existed. He was invented by the owner and editor of the *Monthly Miscellany*, James Pettifer. Presumably it was a slow news day. It certainly explains why Fonte, who is meant to have been an admiral, shows more interest in keeping his larder stocked than in, for instance, reporting information for the cartographers back in Spain.

However, Jefferys doesn't have that excuse. Looking at his maps makes one feel that the king could have done rather better in his choice of mapmaker. Jefferys's map of America still included the city of Cibola in New Mexico[3] and the country of Quivira in what is now (roughly speaking) Kansas. Both, it almost goes without saying, were meant to be fabulously wealthy and both had been revealed to be fantasies by the same man, Francisco Vanquez de Coronado, during his expedition of 1539–42 – that is, some 200 years before Jefferys put pen to paper.

Then there was the North Pole, where Jefferys followed the centuries-old practice of filling it in not, as one might think was already apparent from the many European voyages skirting the Arctic, as an area of ice, but as the Tartarian Sea,[3] in which sit four temperate islands, one of which is identified as a nation of dwarfs.

3. Anyone wondering why the Arctic was apparently being confused here with either Central Asia or Crimea, which is (roughly) what the term 'Tartary' has usually meant, may be comforted to learn that the Greeks used it to describe the lands to the east and north of the world known to them. Still, that was some time before Jefferys.

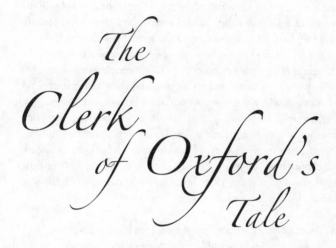

The
Clerk
of Oxford's
Tale

A friend of Chaucer's discovers the Arctic

Chaucer, Hakluyt, Columbus, Mercator, Dee – great names to conjure with – a poet, a scholar, an explorer, a mapmaker and an alchemist, each a master of his art. They are brought together by the almost invisible figure of a medieval friar named Nicholas of Lynn and his no less shadowy work, the *Inventio Fortunata*.

We begin with Dee, a one-man Renaissance, whose interests ranged from the absurdities of alchemy to mathematics, astronomy, geography and all points in between. He was also a keen propagandist for Elizabeth I, who, like his Queen, wished to see

England build its own empire to rival the Spanish.

It is against this background that a letter from Mercator to Dee, written in 1577, comes to notice. In it Mercator makes one of only two known references to the *Inventio Fortunata*. Not that Mercator had seen it, for, he wrote, it had been lost, but he had read of it in the travels of a Belgian called Jacob Cnoyen. Unfortunately, Mercator could no longer locate the copy of Cnoyen's book that he had seen either; and neither has anyone else been able to since. It might be thought that for such a manuscript to be lost once is a misfortune, but for it to be lost twice smacks a little too much of convenience. Yet Mercator, surely, was too serious-minded to invent such things.

Certainly, he didn't invent the *Inventio Fortunata*, although whether it ever had existed is another matter. Columbus, for one, thought that it did. A letter to him from one John Day, an English merchant employed by the Spanish, and dated to late 1497 or early 1498, was discovered in 1956. In it Day apologizes for not being able to fulfil Columbus's wishes:

> Your Lordship's servant brought me your letter. I have seen
> its contents, and I would be most desirous and most happy to
> serve you. I do not find the book *Inventio Fortunata*, and I
> thought that I – or he – was bringing it with my things. I am
> very sorry not [to] find it.

This suggests that Day had owned, or procured at Columbus's request, a copy of the work, but, like Mercator later, had mislaid it. There is nothing to imply that the book was particularly rare (and in the next sentence Day discusses Marco Polo in much the same context).

Aside from that there is a fog of silence, although the fact that there are a good number of maps from this period with the same strange configuration at the North Pole – used by Jefferys 300 years later – points to the conclusion that knowledge of the *Inventio Fortunata* or of its findings was widespread. We must assume, then, that what little remains on the record is a tantalizing glimpse of a vanished history, and not of a work that existed only in fantasy.

In pursuit of Dee's attempts to conjure an empire for his Queen, Mercator revealed to him that in AD 530 no less illustrious a predecessor of the Virgin Queen than King Arthur himself had sent a 4,000-strong expedition to conquer the lands at the North Pole.[1] The vast majority of the men on this venture had perished in the whirlpool that lay at the Pole itself, nestled between the four temperate islands, which, thanks to Mercator's and others' reading of Cnoyen, would grace maps of the polar regions for some 200 years.[2] 'The water rushes round and descends into the earth just as if one were pouring it through a filter funnel,' says Mercator. It is the inverse of the four rivers of the Earthly Paradise.[3] The difference is that at the heart of the whirlpool,[4] right beneath the Pole itself, there is a vast lodestone, glistening and black, called the Rupes Negre, which reaches beyond sight into the sky. It is to this point that all the compasses of the world bend.

In 1360, Mercator relates, in the reign of Edward III, an unnamed Oxford Franciscan, also an astronomer and mathematician, sailed with a number of other men to the far north. There he left his companions and travelled on alone, relying on his 'magic arts' and his astrolabe for his survival, measuring and mapping as he went. After he returned to England he wrote an account of his discoveries in the polar regions and presented it to his king. Thus was the *Inventio Fortunata* born.

1. This is from Cnoyen. It will come as no surprise that Cnoyen's source for this, the *Res Gestae Arturi Britanni*, is also lost.
2. See the Spanish Admiral's Tale.
3. See the Orientalists' Tales.
4. It seems plausible that the whirlpool at least has its roots in sailors' tales of Corryvreckan, the great and lethal whirlpool off the coast of the Hebridean island of Jura. It certainly seems to be Corryvreckan to which the historian Gerald of Wales, writing in the late 12th or early 13th century is referring in this passage: 'Not far from [the Hebrides] towards the north there is a certain wonderful whirlpool of the sea, whereinto all the waves of the sea from far have their course and recourse, as it were without stop. Which, there conveying themselves into the secret receptacles of nature, are swallowed up, as it were, into a bottomless pit, and if it chance that any ship do pass this way, it is pulled, and drawn with such a violence of the waves, that soon without remedy, the force of the whirlpool devours the same.' Mercator, it should be said, did not agree. He cited the same text in support of the polar whirlpool.

Four years later eight men arrived as if from nowhere at the court of the Norwegian king. All claimed to be descendants of members of King Arthur's failed polar colony. Two of them were clerics and one of these had an astrolabe, which he said had been presented to him by the Oxford astronomer in return for a Bible. It was here that Cnoyen met them and first learned of the friar's strange journey.

But it was Hakluyt who moved the story on: when he printed a version of it, courtesy of Dee, he stated that the Franciscan in question was Nicholas of Lynn. Little is known about Nicholas, other than that he was a contemporary of Chaucer's, that he had studied at Oxford, and that he was indeed a noted astronomer and mathematician. It is possible that the two men were acquainted. Chaucer certainly knew of Nicholas, since he explicitly drew on the latter's work in his own unfinished *Treatise of the Astrolabe*, surely one of the earliest technical manuals in existence and definitely the only one written by a major English poet.

Of Nicholas's character, even less is certain, although there are at least curious grounds for speculation, which are to be found in the least likely place: Chaucer's Miller's Tale. In that story of adultery and lust, Chaucer sketches a Nicholas of his own whose outline is uncannily like that of the man under discussion: he is a clerk from Oxford with an interest in the astrolabe and obsession with the stars… As for his other traits, we can only wonder.

The
Survivor's
Tale

A '*dear little island*' in the Pacific proves hostile
to settlers and shipping alike

Our friend Benjamin Morrell (last glimpsed in the
Mapmakers' Tales) crops up again in connection
with another group of islands in sub-Antarctic
waters, the Auckland Islands, some 300 miles south of New Zealand.

The archipelago had been discovered in August 1806 by
Abraham Bristow, captain of the *Ocean*, a whaling vessel.
Unfortunately, owing partly to the vagaries of navigation and partly
to the hostility of the seas so far south, the islands were placed on the
maps some 35 miles adrift of their true location.

In any event, Morrell didn't seem to have any trouble finding
them, dropping anchor at the main island of the group – or so he later

claimed – in January 1830. On the evidence he presented, the island was a picturesque idyll, 'a delightful retreat to a few amiable families who wish for "a dear little isle of their own"'. The climate was balmy and mild, the woods and valleys as green in winter as in summer. All kinds of livestock would thrive, he said, be they 'bullocks, horses, sheep, goats, hogs, foxes, rabbits, geese, ducks [or] poultry of all kinds', and grain, fruits and vegetables 'could be made to flourish here with very little labour'. There was no island in the world of similar size, he continued, with as many safe, good harbours. He even picked out a site for a village. 'On the whole,' he summarized, 'I think that Auckland's [sic] Island is one of the finest places for a small settlement that can be found on any island in the southern hemisphere above the latitude of 35 degrees.'

It was this sort of talk, no doubt, that led Britain, its empire confidently bestriding the world, to start a settlement on the Auckland Islands. In December 1849 some 150 plucky prospective settlers – men, women and children – arrived at Port Ross, to the north of Auckland Island.

Unfortunately, and contrary to Morrell's encomium, the weather was somewhat less than pleasant. Rare was the day when it didn't rain; the winds were usually gale force or stronger; and the temperature struggled to see the north side of 15º Celsius. No wonder Morrell earned himself a dubious reputation. By August 1852 – pluckiness be damned – the last of the colonists had left. It was, arguably, the shortest-lived colony in the history of the empire.

Certainly, his hyperbole about the island's natural harbours was no better placed. It is said that at one point there were so many shipwrecks that the islands were checked twice a year for castaways just on the off chance.

In January 1864, for instance, Captain Musgrave, sailing the *Grafton* out of Sydney, found his ship caught in a ferocious storm. He sought refuge in Carnley Harbour, a lagoon in which Morrell had (or claimed to have) anchored, which lies between Auckland Island itself and its close neighbour to the south, Adams Island. Like much of the archipelago, the harbour lies between steep basalt cliffs. In this particular storm the rock walls served merely to funnel the fury of the winds, driving the helpless *Grafton* past what are now known as Musgrave Peninsula and Musgrave Harbour until it ran aground. Five men, including the captain, survived on Auckland Island until July 1865. Having done what little could be done to prepare the *Grafton's* boat, Musgrave took his mate and one other crew member out onto the open sea. Two crewmen were left behind on the promise that Musgrave and his men would return – assuming that they would themselves survive the voyage back to civilization. It must have seemed a thin promise to hang hopes on. Musgrave and his companions were fortunate, however. Some six days later they found themselves in the aptly named Port Adventure on Stewart Island, 300-odd miles to the north and about 15 miles south of New Zealand's South Island. From there Musgrave was taken to Invercargill on the mainland, where he raised enough money and provisions to return to the Auckland Islands and liberate his two remaining crewmen.

Extraordinarily, however, Musgrave and his men had not been alone. From 10 May 1864 to 22 May 1865, entirely unbeknownst to them, they had shared the island with the survivors of another wreck, that of the *Invercauld*. This ship had been broken by the island's sheer western cliffs. There had been 25 on board, of whom 19 struggled to shore, where they starved, some even resorting to cannibalism.[1] As if things weren't bad enough for the two bands of survivors, May 1864 saw an earthquake on the island. Only three of the 19 from the *Invercauld* survived, including its captain, George Delgarno.

The following year, on 14 May 1866, the *General Grant*, an American ship registered in Boston, was a week out of Melbourne, bound for London, when it went down, another victim of the island's western reaches. There were 83 on board, mostly women and children.

It was a foggy night and the captain was attempting the steer the *General Grant* between the mainland and Disappointment Island[2], some six miles offshore. But the wind was falling away and with it, in

1. One suspects that if the Panglossian Captain Morrell had been among them, he would have been the first to be put in the pot.
2. The *Dundonald* was wrecked on this charmingly named island in 1907. The survivors waited eight months to be rescued.

the age of sail, went the captain's ability to control his ship. Soon there was dead calm and the swell of the sea was driving them closer to the rocks of Auckland Island. By now it was midnight. If there were any hope that the current, setting northward, might clear the ship of the island, it would soon be snuffed out. The ship's jib boom, a spar projecting out from its bow and securing the triangular jib sails to the foremast, smashed into a rock dead ahead. With the jibs gone, the captain lost much of his ability to manouever. The *General Grant* twisted round and smacked its stern into a cave entrance, crushing the rudder; the shock was so brutal it injured the man at the wheel. The ship scraped against the sheer cliffs; looking out, its passengers could just make out the black mass of the rocks rising up out of the darkness. It was around 1.30 am.

Lamps were held over the ship's side, but there was nowhere to set down, barely even a foothold. The captain ordered soundings taken; the sea floor lay 25 fathoms beneath the stern. All the while, the current was driving the *General Grant* further into the cave, loosened rocks and sections of spar splitting off and crashing into the cold black sea below. Overhanging rocks in the cave roof ripped down three of the ship's masts in quick succession, and the jagged wooden stumps that remained brought further rockfalls smashing down onto the ship's deck, smashing right through the fore deck and the starboard deckhouse, the sound booming around the dark cave, while the passengers huddled, terrified, at the stern of the ship awaiting the captain's order to launch the boats. But the sea, at least, was calm in the cave, and the captain wanted to wait for daybreak.

Daylight broke with another mast brought down and the captain ordered the boats made ready. There were three on board, two 22-footers and a 30-foot longboat. The first smaller boat was launched over the stern, with a line and a makeshift anchor. The intention was for this boat to drop the anchor outside the cave and return to pick up more passengers, hauling their way to safety along the line. But there was some confusion and the boat simply lay outside, waiting, as the sea grew wilder – both inside and outside the cave.

The second smaller boat was made ready. Into it first went beef and pork and fifty tins of stew. Then, the captain planned, would go the women and children. But the sea was getting up and only one woman, a Mrs Jewell, could make the leap into the cold water, a rope fastened about her, before the waves got too high. She and four others were ferried to the first boat, the second returning to the ship.

But things were moving quickly now. The ship's main mast had been driven through the hull by the overhanging rocks. The third and largest boat still lay on the deck, packed with passengers, while the *General Grant* sank beneath it. It floated free of the deck, but the second boat couldn't get close enough to help. They watched as, some 100 yards from the wreck, the longboat, no doubt low in the water with the weight of people it carried, was swamped by a wave and sank. Only three could be saved, all strong swimmers.

Looking back to the ship in the cave, the survivors could still make out the figure of the captain, high in the mizzen-topmast crosstrees. Some of the men knew, without seeing, that their wives were still on board, too. But in a few minutes, as the sea broke heavily on the rocks and the wind rose, there was nothing left to be seen at all.

Above them stood some 400 feet of cliffs, with no hope of landfall. They decided to make for Disappointment Island,[3] about six miles away to the west. They toiled all day, bailing desperately as they went every second of the way, the boat sometimes all but full of water. Finally they gave up and decided to let the current take then to whatever rocks it would, but as they drifted they felt the weather lift and, spying a large rock a mile or so distant off the shore of Disappointment Island, they pulled hard for that. At nightfall, with the storm abating, they made it.

Only 15 survived the wreck and made it ashore. They were

3. On a lighter note, the naming of new lands usually represented a chance to flatter the rich and powerful, or else reward friends and comrades. Names with more intrinsic interest, such as this one, are few and far between. Certainly, very few manage to do it with the style of Luke Foxe, an independent-minded Jacobean sailor, who named one island off North America Sir Thomas Roe's Welcome and gave another small archipelago the wholly splendid name Brigges His Mathematickes. Sadly, the latter hasn't lasted on the maps, although the former is still applied to an inlet. (While on the subject of names, one can't help being amused by the fact that there is an island off the coast of Greenland called Disco Island and another, further west towards Newfoundland, called Funk Island.)

stranded for 18 months. In January the following year four of the men were lost attempting to sail, as Musgrave had done, to New Zealand in a small boat. Eventually, the *Amherst*, a whaler, out of Invercargill, New Zealand, rescued the remaining ten survivors – another had died on the island – on 21 November 1867.

The Utopians' Tales

*The man who gave his name to the Americas sees strange
things off their shores*

*U*sually reports of monsters and other prodigies of
nature were safely made at second or third hand.
One exception to this rule is contained in a letter
written by Amerigo Vespucci on his second voyage to the continents
that would bear his name, in 1499–1500. Describing Curaçao, he
recalled walking along the beach and seeing huge human footprints
in the wet sand. Reckoning that such a small island could not support
a large population, particularly of people so big, he and his men
explored the hinterland further. Within four miles of the coast they
stumbled across a few huts. Five giant women sat before them.
Vespucci and his men moved to kidnap three of the women, but some

30 giant men, armed with clubs and bows and arrows, arrived before they could put the plan into action. The giants chased them to their ship and, watching Vespucci's men embark, began to shoot at them. In return the Europeans fired a handful of mortars and the giants melted away. The voyage's cartographer, Juan de la Cosa, who had also sailed on some of Columbus's voyages, dutifully recorded the Island of Giants on his map, the first European map of the New World.

Also on this voyage – almost certainly, anyway – was Ralph Hythloday, the Portuguese sailor who appears as Thomas More's chief informant in his *Utopia* (1515). More reports that Hythloday was on three of Vespucci's four voyages, but, on the last, he insisted that he and 23 colleagues be set ashore 'at the farthest place at which they touched'. Sadly More is less specific about the location of Utopia, although he does, perhaps with pygmies and giants in mind, have Hythloday reveal that 'we made no inquiries after monsters, than which nothing is more common; for everywhere one may hear of ravenous dogs and wolves, and cruel men-eaters, but it is not so easy to find states that are well and wisely governed.'

Francis Bacon, meanwhile, in his *New Atlantis*, written a century or so later, is more forthcoming about the location of his perfect realm. But then, he had the advantage of Hakluyt's publication of innumerable narratives of real voyages in the interim. They gave something of their tone to Bacon's fiction, which starts as follows:

We sailed from Peru, where we had continued by the space of one whole year, for China and Japan, by the South Sea, taking with us victuals for twelve months; and had good winds from the east, though soft and weak, for five months' space and more. But then the wind came about, and settled in the west for many days, so as we could make little or no way, and were sometime in purpose to turn back. But then again there arose strong and great winds from the south, with a point east; which carried us up. for all that we could do, toward the north: by which time our victuals failed us, though we had made good spare of them. So that finding ourselves in the midst of the greatest wilderness of waters in the world, without victuals, we gave ourselves for lost men, and prepared for death. Yet we did lift up our hearts and voices to God above, who showeth His wonders in the deep, beseeching Him of His mercy that as in the beginning He discovered the face of the deep, and brought forth dry land, so He would now discover land to us, that we might not perish.

And it came to pass that the next day about evening we saw within a kenning before us, toward the north, as it were thick clouds, which did put us in some hope of land, knowing how that part of the South Sea was utterly unknown, and might have islands or continents that hitherto were not come to light. Wherefore we bent our course thither, where we saw the appearance of land, all that night; and in the dawning of the next day we might plainly discern that it was a land flat to our sight, and full of boscage, which made it show the more dark. And after an hour and a half's sailing, we entered into a good haven, being the port of a fair city; not great indeed, but well built, and that gave a pleasant view from the sea: and we thinking every minute long till we were on land, came close to the shore and offered to land...

The
Sea Captain's
Tale

*A roguish captain makes things difficult
for mapmakers*

Returning from Frobisher's third voyage to Meta Incognita in 1578, one of the ships, the small *Emmanuel* from Bridgwater in Somerset – a vessel first designed for the herring industry and of a kind known as a 'buss' – was caught in a storm before it had got out into the open sea. The rest of the fleet, driven by the wind, sailed on over the horizon while the crew of the *Emmanuel* attempted to ride the storm out, anchoring it hazardously as close to shore as the men dared go.

The next day, 3 September, was clear, with the winds north-northwest. The men weighed anchor and made it to Friesland – in actual fact, the southern part of Greenland – which had been renamed 'West England' on the voyage over, by the evening of the 8th. From there, despite changeable winds, they steered south-southeast until the 12th. That day, around 11 am, the men on deck sighted land about five leagues to the east. It was an island, some 25 leagues in length, large enough to remain in plain view for over 24 hours. The surrounding sea was thick with ice, however, which made it impossible to land, despite the fact that they could descry what looked like at least two harbours on the coast. George Best, one of those sailing on the *Emmanuel*, wrote of 'the land seeming to be fruitful, full of woods and a champion country'. It was a couple of days before the seas were clear of ice and the men of the *Emmanuel* continued for home, which they caught first sight of some 12 days later.

The island was not formally given a name, but it became known as Buss Island and it is under that soubriquet that it appears on a map for the first time: the famous Molyneux globe of 1592. It was seen again in 1606 by James Hall on his way to Greenland, but the abundant ice prevented him, too, from landing. After that the trail went cold for 60-odd years, until a Captain Zachariah Gillam saw the island while en route for Hudson Bay in 1668.

Three years later came the first recorded landfall. As noted in Sellers's *English Pilot*, the definitive navigational book for English seamen of the period:

This island was further discovered by Captain Thomas
Shepherd in the *Golden Lion* of Dunkirk in the year 1671…
The said Captain Shepherd brought home the map of the
island… and he reports that the island affords store of whales,
easy to be struck, sea-horse, seal, and cod in abundance, and
he supposes that two voyages may be made in a year. The sea
is clear from ice unless in September. The land is low and
level to the southward, and there are some hills and
mountains on the northwestern end. There lieth a bank about
twelve leagues to the southward of the island, that hath good
store of fish upon it, and is about 15 leagues in length.

This copy was indeed accompanied by Shepherd's detailed and handsome map.

Shepherd, a man whose career had taken him no higher than to the captaincy of fishing vessels, knew when he was onto a good thing. He found 17 features on the island that he could give names to; of these, he named 12 after directors of the Hudson's Bay Company, which had been incorporated the previous May.[1] Perhaps it is a coincidence, but within two years Shepherd was working for them.

It should be said, however, that the historian who has delved into the tale of Buss Island most deeply, Miller Christy, doesn't take such a sanguine view:

> I am inclined to regard [Shepherd's account] as pure
> invention, concocted by a rascally captain who hoped to
> secure either a pecuniary reward or meretricious renown by
> claiming to have actually discovered and explored an island
> which had long been represented on the charts, but of which
> nothing was otherwise known.

It doesn't help Shepherd's case that, from that day to this, no one else has ever laid eyes on Buss Island.

That's not for want of trying. So sure were seamen of the existence of the island that, following the repeated failures to find it, the presumption grew that it must have sunk. Thus, for instance, on Van Keulen's map of 1745 it appears as 'the submerged land of Buss [which] is nowadays nothing but surf, a quarter of a mile long, with a rough sea'.

However, Captain Richard Pickersgill, for one, didn't believe this. If it had sunk,[3] he reasoned, it could hardly have done so without 'so violent a concussion as must have affected the north of Europe'. Considering arguments such as Van Keulen's, he took the view that they had in fact been a hindrance, not a help: 'The seamen in consequence [of hearing about the dangerous seas around the island] instead of endeavouring to discover, use all means in their power to

---

1. Modestly, he named a hitherto unknown island off the shore of Buss after himself.

avoid' Buss Island. Sailing to Hudson Bay in 1776, he took soundings and found shallows in the vicinity. In addition, he reported seamen's gossip: a Greenlander had been alarmed by breakers there and found rock at 39 fathoms; a Dutch ship had been so beaten by the breakers that it had to return home lest it sank.

John Ross, too, on his way to the Arctic in search of the Northwest Passage,[2] took an interest in the subject, since the island, sunken or not, still appeared on the sea charts. Perhaps it was just idle curiosity. It was Sunday 17 May 1818, a beautiful day, he reported. Service had been performed and the ship's watch had been divided to allow the men much more leisure time than was customary. At noon, finding themselves at the right latitude, they resolved to find out the truth once and for all. They changed direction and sailed towards the sunken land of Buss, their eyes scanning the horizon. At sunset they shortened the sails and hove to; taking soundings, they could find no bottom in 180 fathoms. They repeated the exercise every four miles, but the result was the same. Ross talked to his crew:

> Various stories respecting it were related by people on board,
> but it appeared, on comparing their testimonies, that no
> soundings had ever actually been found. I am more inclined
> to imagine that when ships have been struck in this quarter
> by heavy seas, the shocks have erroneously been attributed to
> the sunken land of Buss.

And with those words the island sank from view entirely.

In some ways, this is a shame, since sunken islands are not a wholly unreasonable conjecture. It's certainly not as far-fetched as the floating islands that seem to have hovered around the edges of geography and history since classical times. As is often the case, Herodotus was one of the first to report their existence. Although he does so charmingly – and slightly out of character – even he is sceptical. He writes of an island called Chemmis where 'there is a great temple-house of Apollo, and three several altars are set up within,

2. See the Officers' Tales.

and there are planted in the island many palm-trees and other trees, both bearing fruit and not bearing fruit'. The island itself is said to be 'in a deep and broad lake by the side of the temple at Buto, and it is said by the Egyptians that this island is a floating island. I myself did not see it either floating about or moved from its place, and I feel surprise at hearing of it, wondering if it be indeed a floating island.' Plutarch later took up Herodotus's baton and wrote that Chemmis not only floated, but also drifted quite considerably, having been seen at various points along the Nile and, indeed, out at sea. That is where most floating islands have tended to be noticed, or imagined. There is, for instance, As-Sayyâra, described in an anonymous 10th-century book of marvels, which, because its rocks are light and airy, simply drifts along with the wind. Floating islands have also been reported among the Faeroes and – by Columbus no less – the Canaries. There is also Perdita, the 'lost' island, as noted in the medieval *De imagine mundi*, which, beautiful as it is, can never be found by anyone seeking it, but only by those who happen across it by chance.

The Courtier's Tale

Sir Walter Raleigh searches for
El Dorado up the Orinoco River

S ome time in the 1580s – probably during the autumn of
1586 – Sir Walter Raleigh had an opportunity to discuss
the Straits of Magellan with a Spanish conquistador by the
name of Don Pedro de Sarmiento. Raleigh, thirsty for knowledge,
wanted to know everything. He couldn't have had a better inter-
locutor: Sarmiento's experience of South America stretched back 30
years. No doubt they had a map open in front of them, for at one
point Raleigh asked Sarmiento about a particular island in the
Straits. Sarmiento laughed. 'It was,' Raleigh remembered him saying,
'to be called the Painter's Wife's Island… While the fellow drew that
map,' he continued, 'his wife, sitting by, desired to put in one coun-

try for her; that she, in imagination, might have an island of her own.'[1]

If ever a man failed to learn the lesson of the story of the painter's wife, it was Sir Walter Raleigh. Within ten years of hearing it from Sarmiento he was to be found struggling up the Orinoco River in search of El Dorado, the fabled city of gold, which hadn't even made it onto a map.

To be fair, Sarmiento himself may have been partly to blame. It was from him that Raleigh first heard the story of 'that mighty, rich, and beautiful empire of Guiana, and of that great and golden city, which the Spaniards call El Dorado, and the naturals [natives] Manoa'. The problem was that, even in the 1570s, El Dorado was fairly old hat and by the 1580s it was passing into oblivion. Without Raleigh most of us would never had heard of it, just as most of us have never heard of Paititi, or Cibola, or Quivira – all rumoured cities or lands of fabulous wealth that the Spanish went haring around Central and South America in search of.[2]

In 1539 Gonzales Pizarro, younger brother of the legendary conquistador, had led an expedition across the Andes out of Quito in Peru, searching for both the golden city and cinnamon trees. He and

1. The 17th-century historian Peter Heylyn, noting this exchange in his *Cosmography* (1659), added: 'I fear the Painter's Wife hath many islands – and some countries, too – upon the continent of our common maps which are not really to be found on the strictest search.'
2. There is a school of thought that says that all such stories derive from the Native Americans' insight that the best way to get rid of their new Christian acquaintances was to tell them stories about great stores of gold somewhere else – and preferably somewhere a very great distance from wherever they happened to be. Saguenay is a good example (see the Native's Tale). Europeans could also be experts at self-delusion. In 1539 Friar Marcos de Niza, exploring to the north of Mexico with his North African companion Esteban, discovered the city of Cibola, after, it must be said, much foreshadowing by his native guides. 'It is situated', he reported, ' on a plain at the foot of a round hill, and seems a fair city, better than any I have seen in these parts. The houses are well-ordered, as the Indians had told me, built of stone, several storeys high, and with flat roofs – as far as I could tell from the mountainside which I had climbed to get a better view. The people are somewhat white, they wear clothes and lie in beds, and use bows as weapons. They have emeralds and other jewels, although they prefer

his men sailed down the Marañón River to where it meets the Napo. At this point a party under Gonzales Pizarro's lieutenant Francisco de Orellana, which had been scouting ahead for supplies, became separated from the main group. It was 26 December 1541. Unable to return upstream, Orellana continued to drift with the current down to the Atlantic. Later his party reported that the Amazon basin was heavily populated, with great towns and villages at once terrible and beautiful, glimmering white houses, and riverbanks lined with human heads. Along the way, on 24 June 1542, one of Orellana's raiding parties was itself attacked by natives, who, they reported, were led by a caste of female warriors. Orellana thought immediately of the Amazons of classical mythology[3] and thus the river got a new name. It wasn't until 26 August, eight months after they had lost sight of their comrades, that Orellana and his men finally saw the ocean. According to Raleigh, at least, having discounted the Amazon as the location of El Dorado Orellana had won permission, before he died in 1546, to return to the region and look elsewhere.

Then there was the notorious Lope de Aguirre. In 1558 he served as a junior officer in Pedro de Urzúa's expedition to explore the headwaters of the Amazon, looking for El Dorado in the lands of the

---

turquoises, with which they decorate the walls and porches of their houses – as well as their clothes – and which they also use in place of money. The clothes they wear are made of cotton and ox-hide. They use vessels of gold and silver, since they have no other metals, and both are more abundant than in Peru…' There were seven cities like this, Niza was told, and this was the least of them. The next year he guided a Spanish expedition under Francisco Vazquez de Coronado to the site. The army was unamused to find no more than seven Pueblo villages, and Niza was disgraced. Coronado, however, went on to discover the Grand Canyon.

3. See the Amazons' Tales. Raleigh, meanwhile, made his own investigations among the local tribes. His sources told him that the Amazons 'which are not far from Guiana do accompany with men but once in a year, and for the time of one month,' he told us. He gathered that the month in question was April. 'At that time, all kings of the borders assemble, and queens of the Amazons; and after the queens have chosen, the rest cast lots for their valentines', a charming if implausible detail. 'This one month they feast, dance, and drink of their wines in abundance; and the moon being done they all depart to their own provinces. They are said to be very cruel and bloodthirsty, especially to such as offer to invade their territories. [They] have likewise great store of these plates of gold…'

rebellious Omagua people. The men were exhausted and starving, and Aguirre led a revolt against Urzúa and slew him. The same fate awaited Urzúa's successor, Fernando de Guzmán, whom Aguirre found insufficiently tractable. Aguirre then took command of the 700 men who remained loyal to him, had the rest slaughtered, and set out to make himself Emperor of Guiana and Peru. He came down to the Atlantic coast, 'spoiling all the coast of Caracas and the province of Venezuela and of Rio de la Hacha', in Raleigh's phrase.[4] Aguirre's approach was simple: anyone who didn't recognize his authority would die. It is said, not least by Raleigh himself, that when Aguirre was finally cornered he killed his own children: not being able to make them princes, he said, he would ensure they wouldn't have to endure the shame of having had a traitor for a father.[5]

The strange thing is that Raleigh knew most of this before he set out for South America. Indeed, he collected these stories and more besides in his book *The Discovery of Guiana*. Most of the tales end in death, all of them in disappointment. Yet still he set out, drawn on by the prospect of gold and glory,[6] and, of course, by hostility to the Spanish. Their conquests were almost a personal affront to men like Raleigh who believed in the providential destiny of Protestant England. 'We find that by the abundant treasure of [South America]' Raleigh fumed, 'the Spanish king vexes all the princes of Europe, and is become, in a few years, from a poor king of Castile, the greatest

4. Raleigh recalled, erroneously, it seems, given the dates, that Sir John Hawkins had met Aguirre – 'such a one upon the coast who rebelled and had sailed down the Amazon' – on his voyage in the *Jesus of Lubeck*, when he had been forced to leave more than 100 of his men to their fate in the Gulf of Mexico. See the Drunkard's Tale.

5. The *Encyclopaedia Britannica*, looking for words to describe this man, who left a trail of blood and betrayal through the region, settles for 'thoroughly disreputable', which seems a generous assessment to say the least.

6. Raleigh liked glory. He 'esteemed more of fame than of conscience,' notes Ben Jonson, who knew him well. Jonson was tutor to Raleigh's son Wat, whom he accompanied on a visit to Paris and Brussels in 1613. In Paris Jonson drank himself insensible and, in that state, allowed Wat to have him tied, in the shape of a cross, onto a barrow and wheel him around the town. The point was to mock Catholic idolatry. Wat, it seems, liked to live dangerously. Raleigh, who held his own dignity in high esteem, was livid when he heard; his wife Bess, however, thought it was rather funny.

monarch of this part of the world.' Raleigh believed that with the acquisition of El Dorado he would have a way 'to answer every man's longing,' which was, to his mind at least, 'a better Indies for her Majesty than the king of Spain hath'.

Of course, the painter's wife notwithstanding, the fact that there was nothing but hearsay to go on shouldn't necessarily have discouraged Raleigh. After all, Pizarro had barely even had that much to go on when they stumbled across the Inca empire, 70-odd years before. There's little doubt that it was the likes of the Pizarros in Peru and of Cortés in Mexico that Raleigh sought to emulate. Just look at the full title of the book he wrote about his search for El Dorado, already mentioned above:

The Discovery of the large, rich, and beautiful Empire of Guiana; with a relation of the great and golden city of Manoa, which the Spaniards call El Dorado, and the provinces of Emeria, Aromaia, Amapaia, and other countries, with their rivers, adjoining. Performed in the year 1595 by Sir Walter Raleigh, Knight, Captain of her Majesty's Guard, Lord Warden of the Stannaries and her Highness's Lieutenant General of the County of Cornwall.

Anyone coming across the volume on the bookstands in 1596 could have been forgiven for thinking that Raleigh had actually found something.

The truth, of course, was somewhat different. As our notional bookbuyer would have realized once he got *The Discovery of Guiana* home and found, perhaps after lighting a Raleighesque pipe of best tobacco, that it begins with an apology, about 4,000 words long – or rather a sort of apology, laced with bluster and self-justification. One can well imagine that if either of the book's two dedicatees – Sir Charles Howard, Baron Effingham and Lord High Admiral, or Sir Robert Cecil, son of Lord Burleigh and the Queen's Secretary of State – ever perused the book, they would have thought that Raleigh had much to be sorry about. 'I have hitherto only returned promises,' Raleigh says to them, 'and now, for answer of both your adventures, I

Mathew Lyons

have sent you a bundle of papers.' That probably wasn't exactly what they were after. Howard and Cecil were spending political capital on supporting Raleigh's exploits, given that he had been in extreme disfavour with the Queen since she'd discovered three years before that Raleigh had secretly married one of her ladies-in-waiting, Bess Throckmorton. Elizabeth had responded to this crisis with her usual caution and calm: she had had husband and wife both thrown into the Tower of London.

Others, who had spent rather more tangible kinds of capital, were no doubt keen to hear from Raleigh, too. His expedition had been funded to the vast and extraordinary tune of £60,000, a sum roughly equivalent to one third of the government's own revenue. By way of comparison, Frobisher's first voyage to find the Northwest Passage, back in 1576, had cost £875, itself not a small amount. A bundle of papers wasn't exactly the kind of return to kindle warmth in anyone's heart. By the time Raleigh gets around to mentioning 'the great debt which I have no power to pay' a few lines later, the truth would well and truly have sunk in for everyone: Raleigh was a man who couldn't help but do everything on a heroic scale, including defaulting on loans.

It's clear, though, that plenty of his countrymen thought that Raleigh lied on an epic scale, too. Raleigh says, with what reads very like petulance, that:

I was never hidden in Cornwall, or elsewhere, as was supposed. They have grossly belied me that forejudged that I would rather become a servant to the Spanish king than return; and the rest were much mistaken, who would have persuaded that I was too easeful and sensual to undertake a journey of so great travail.

As for the samples of gold ore that he had managed to bring back, there was no shortage of detractors on hand to belittle him about those too. Some claimed that it was merely fool's gold. Others, as Raleigh noted, said that he had simply bought the ore on the Barbary Coast and taken it with him to Guiana. His tart response was this:

182

Surely the singularity of that device I do not well
comprehend. For mine own part, I am not so much in love
with these long voyages as to devise thereby to cozen myself,
to lie hard, to fare worse, to be subjected to perils, to diseases,
to ill savours, to be parched and withered, and withal to
sustain the care and labour of such an enterprise, except the
same had more comfort than the fetching of marcasite in
Guiana, or buying of gold ore in Barbary.

It's hard not to feel that, here at least, he had a point.

Having come back more or less empty-handed, Raleigh knew that
he had to draw on all his talent for grandiose writing to persuade cyn-
ical, disgruntled and, in some cases, probably suddenly impoverished
readers that his failure had in fact been a noble success. His strategy
for doing so, which we shall come to later, was quite brilliant. In the
meantime, though, he knew what his readers wanted.

First of all, they expected stories of gold and treasure and English
greatness:

The country hath more quantity of gold, by manifold, than
the best parts of the Indies, or Peru. All the most of the kings
of the borders are already become her Majesty's vassals, and
seem to desire nothing more than her Majesty's protection
and the return of the English nation. It hath another ground
and assurance of riches and glory than the voyages of the
West Indies; an easier way to invade the best parts thereof
than by the common course.

Second, they were hungry for a taste of the strange new world that
they would never have a chance to see for themselves. Accordingly,
in a bravura piece of appetite-whetting, Raleigh manages to name-
check about 50 places in a single paragraph, the rich exotic syllables
in themselves seeming to promise a kind of luxury:

The cities of Barquasimeta, Valencia, St Sebastian, Cororo,
St Lucia, Laguna, Maracaiba and Truxillo … the Rivers of

Hacha, St Martha, and Carthagena... the ports of Nuevo
Reyno and Popayan... [the] rich and prosperous... towns and
cities of Merida, Lagrita, St Christophoro, the great cities of
Pamplona, Santa Fe de Bogota, Tunxa and Mozo, where the
emeralds are found, the towns and cities of Marequita, Velez,
la Villa de Leiva, Palma, Honda, Angostura, the great city of
Timana, Tocaima, St Aguila, Pasto, [St] Iago, the great city of
Popayan itself, Los Remedios, and the rest... the ports and
villages within the bay of Uraba in the kingdom or rivers of
Darien and Caribana... the cities and towns of St Juan de
Rodas, of Cassaris, of Antiochia, Caramanta, Cali and
Anserma ... Nombre de Dios and Panama ... in the province
of Castilla del Oro... the villages upon the rivers of Cenu
and Chagre; Peru hath, besides those, and besides the
magnificent cities of Quito and Lima, so many islands, ports,
cities and mines as, if I should name them with the rest, it
would seem incredible to the reader.

While this whets the appetite, it also lays down a marker. This fecundity, these riches, may seem incredible to you, Raleigh is saying, but I know that they are real, for I have been there, I have seen with my own eyes and heard with my own ears. You will have to trust my word...

On 22 March 1595 Raleigh had reached the New World at last. He had financed many voyages over the previous 12 years, including the one that led to the creation of the failed colony of Roanoke in the Carolinas, but this was his first direct encounter. He had recently turned 40. He was, perhaps, becoming soft around the edges now, used to comfort and luxury. He and his men had arrived at Trinidad, and then sailed up and down the coast, but they encountered no one, despite spying fires among the trees. The natives, he surmised, were too afraid of the Spanish to come out of the forest.

Raleigh the newcomer wanted to explore the shoreline for himself, to get a feel for the rivers and watering places, the coves and creeks. It was like being a child again, discovering everything new and untested. He noted some small brooks and a freshwater river; oysters growing on the branches of the trees also caught his eye. There was a lake of pitch, the best he had seen; his men made good their ships. But mostly, Trinidad was rich and fruitful. Raleigh the colonizer eyed it up: its excellent soil, he decided, would be good for growing sugar and ginger. There were deer and boar to be had, along with plentiful fish and fowl. He was careful to show how much he knew and to display his authority, claiming familiarity with such New World crops as maize and cassava. He was also pleased to learn that there was gold in the rivers, though the Spanish didn't care to pan for it, for their goal was Guiana, 'the magazine of all rich metals' and sifting grains from the cool water was small beer. Raleigh, it seems, felt the same; he doesn't mention it again in his book.

Still, Raleigh was, quite literally, just coasting, easing himself in, acclimatizing himself. He had no real interest in Trinidad at all. It was enemy territory, after all, albeit thinly garrisoned. What he now needed was information – about the Spanish, about El Dorado, about South America. He sailed up the coast to Port of Spain, where the English newcomers and the Spanish settlers came face to face for the first time.

All such meetings in the New World were strange. Europeans were caught between fear of the native peoples and of the unknown, and fear of their enemies from the Old World. They cleaved to each other as Christians, as white men, in a pagan world; but they distrusted, even hated, each other in no smaller measure. Both sides were wary. The English, just six years after the defeat of the Armada, were clearly well within Spain's sphere of influence and thousands of miles from home. The Spanish, meanwhile, were few in number and eyed the English, armed and relatively numerous as they were, with caution.

It was the Spanish who made the first move. They signalled a desire to do business, to trade with the English in peace – 'more for doubt of their own strength than for aught else,' says Raleigh, probably correctly. Some of them came on board. Also stealing on board that same evening were two natives whom one of Raleigh's men, Captain Whiddon, had befriended the previous year on a reconnaissance mission for Raleigh. The natives told Whiddon and Raleigh what they knew about the Spaniards' strength.

Soon Raleigh was in his element with the Spanish. They came on board to buy linen and other luxuries, to look upon the English ships, and to talk with fellow Christians. These were not, after all, the great Spanish lords of South and Central America; they were foot-soldiers, weary, homesick and poor. Raleigh the courtier knew how to entertain and how to charm. He had an eye for weakness too. These Spaniards had been without wine for years. He feasted them and made them merry. It turned out that they had heard of Raleigh, so perhaps there was a frisson of celebrity that lured them. To them he was 'Guaterrale', the founder of the Roanoke colony far to the north. They had not heard, however, that the settlers had vanished and the colony had failed, and Roanoke remained part of Raleigh's cover story. He was in transit, he told them, to relieve 'those English which I had planted in Virginia'. His interest in Guiana and its marvels was expressed politely, as one soldier to other soldiers. Thus it was that he learned everything they knew: they boasted of Guiana and its riches, and talked at length of the ways and passages to it.

Perhaps to the surprise of the Spanish, given his stated aim, Raleigh lingered on. Every day, he says in his book, he acquired new information. No doubt it was all useful, though Raleigh seems to have been the kind of person who likes information for its own sake, too. However, the governor of the region, Antonio de Berrio, who happened to be at San José, the notional capital of Trinidad about ten miles inland, was no fool. Berrio sent for more troops, intent on a lethal strike at Raleigh – 'giving me a cassado at parting' as Raleigh puts it. Time was running out.

Revenge on Berrio happened to be one of Raleigh's objectives. The year before Berrio had tricked eight of Whiddon's men to their deaths in an ambush. Yet Raleigh knew that Berrio too was on the trail of El Dorado and wanted to find out what the governor knew before getting his blows in.

Meanwhile, Raleigh was also feeling his way towards new alliances. Despite Berrio's threat that any native who traded with Raleigh would be hanged, drawn and quartered – a threat that, as Raleigh learned later, was followed through in at least two cases – every night there was a visit from natives with most lamentable complaints of [Berrio's] cruelty: that he made the ancient *caciques*, which were lords of the country, to be slaves; that he kept them in chains, and dropped their naked bodies with burning bacon, and such other torments, which I found afterwards to be true.

Raleigh had found himself a *casus belli*, a moral outrage to redress: he would take San José. Raleigh the liberator: it suited his style, his large conception of himself. It suited, too, the way he shaped the struggle between English Protestantism and Spanish Catholicism. It was also, of course, expedient, as Raleigh himself readily admits. In a typically pungent turn of phrase he notes that

To enter Guiana by small boats, to depart 400 or 500 miles from my ships, and to leave a garrison in my back interested in the same enterprise, who also daily expected supplies out of Spain, I should have savoured very much of the ass.

He acts swiftly, with the advantage of surprise. 'I set upon the *corps du garde* in the evening, and put them to the sword,' he writes, quite possibly referring to some of the men he had welcomed on board his ship a few days before. By the morning San José was his. Berrio was now in Raleigh's hands, too. The English then set fire to the handful of wooden buildings that comprised the city. In his book Raleigh says that they did so at the natives' suggestion, as if he himself did not think in such terms.

Before pressing on, Raleigh gathered all the native lords of the island together and delivered an oration about Elizabeth, 'the great *cacique* of the North, a virgin, [who] had more *caciqui* under her than there were trees in that island'. An enemy of the Spanish, their tyranny and their oppression, she had sent Raleigh to free them, 'having freed all the coast of the northern world from their servitude'. He showed them a picture of Elizabeth, 'which they so admired and honoured, as it had been easy to have brought them idolatrous thereof'. Raleigh may have been out of favour at court, but he knew the Queen's weaknesses and had not forgotten how to flatter her.

With Berrio on board his ship, Raleigh was a liberator no longer. The revenger's mask was doffed too. Berrio, Raleigh tells his readers,

is a gentleman well descended… very valiant and liberal… a gentleman of great assuredness, and of a great heart. I used him according to his estate and worth in all things I could, according to the small means I had.

Berrio, like Sarmiento before him, thus became an honoured guest. Like Sarmiento, too, he had been in the New World for a long time and knew a great deal about it. He was touching 70; there can have been little that he had not seen. He was, in short, the kind of man Raleigh admired.

They talked a great deal. Berrio told Raleigh of his own attempts to find El Dorado and perhaps it was during their conversations that Raleigh first heard the story of Juan Martinez. While fleeing from an unjust death sentence, Martinez had, by his own account, been caught by the people of Manoa and taken blindfold to their city, entering it at noon, and travelling 'day till night through the city, and the next day from sun rising to sun setting, ere he came to the palace of Inga'. Martinez claimed to have lived in Manoa for seven months before leaving 'laden with as much gold as [he] could carry', but explained his later conspicuous lack of wealth by asserting that he had been robbed of the gold beyond the borders of Guiana.

Berrio and Raleigh probably swapped other stories too. They seem to have shared the same fascination with, or addiction to, the small fragments of information, gleaned like gold dust, with which they fed their dreams. Perhaps Raleigh told Berrio what had reached his own far-off native land, the West Country of England:

a French ship that came from thence, riding in Falmouth the same year that my ships came first from Virginia [that is, in 1585]; and another this year in Helford, that also came from thence, and had been fourteen months at an anchor in Amazons; which were both very rich.

During those hot evenings aboard Raleigh's ship, as he dined on strange meats beneath unfamiliar stars, with an aged conquistador his guest and himself, he hoped, on the threshold of glory, Raleigh must surely have felt that it was the harbours and inlets of home, of small, cold Cornwall, that were insubstantial, even imaginary.

Berrio had at least one shock in store for Raleigh: El Dorado, he said, was '600 English miles further from the sea than I was made believe it had been'. Whiddon's reconnaissance the year before had clearly been flawed. Raleigh was stunned; it was a long, long way to go up river, with the ships still at anchor in the ocean. His response was simply to sit on the information: 'I kept it from the knowledge of my company, who else would never have been brought to attempt the same,' he says.

Eventually, having learned everything he could from Berrio, Raleigh revealed all to him. It was a dramatic moment, the kind of flourish that Raleigh relished. It was El Dorado he was aiming for after all, as it had been for years. At this news

Berrio was stricken into a great melancholy and sadness, and used all the arguments he could to dissuade me; and also assured the gentlemen of my company that it would be labour lost, and that they should suffer many miseries if they proceeded. And first he delivered that I could not enter any of the rivers with any bark or pinnace, or hardly with any ship's boat, it was so low, sandy and full of flats, and that his companies were daily grounded in their canoes, which drew but twelve inches water. He further said that none of the country would come to speak with us, but would all fly; and if we followed them to their dwellings, they would burn their own towns. And besides that, the way was long, the winter at hand, and that the rivers beginning once to swell, it was impossible to stem the current; and that we could not in those small boats by any means carry victuals for half the time, and that (which indeed most discouraged my company) the kings and lords of all the borders of Guiana had decreed that none of them should trade with any Christians for gold,

because the same would be their own overthrow, and that for
the love of gold the Christians meant to conquer and
dispossess them of all together.

It was a passionate speech, but Raleigh was not to be swayed.
'Many and the most of these I found to be true,' he tells us – 'but yet
I resolved to make trial of whatsoever happened.'

Saying such things, making the grand gesture, came easy to
Raleigh. The next step, launching himself and his men upriver,
proved less straightforward. Their first attempt was on a river with
shoals at its mouth offering nine feet of water at high tide and five
feet at low. The tide was too strong and too brief, however, and they
were beaten back before they could clear the sandbanks. It soon
became clear that they would not be able to take their ships anywhere. They would have to 'run up in our ship's boats, one barge, and
two wherries'. It was a doubtful proposition and a nice judgement to
make. Berrio announced that the Spanish would soon be back to
avenge San José. He could hardly be doubted. Neither part of
Raleigh's expedition – those who had gone inland or those who
remained on the coast – could feel safe. Raleigh assured those he left
behind that he would be gone for no more than 15 days, but he knew
that this was untrue.

A local *cacique* then told the Englishmen about other inlets, further east, and Raleigh quickly sent one of his men to scout them out.
He found four good entrances, 'the least as big as the Thames at
Woolwich', but again the bay offered them shoals and six feet of
water, and the ships could not pass. Instead they had to take a mot-
ley collection of craft with them, including an old *gallego* – a small
galleon – that must have been in poor repair, since they had been on
the verge of scuppering it. The carpenters now refitted it as a galley
and they squeezed 60 men into it, Raleigh among them. Alongside
the *gallego* went two wherries, a barge and a ship's boat, each carrying
another ten men. Food and weapons were crowded into all five vessels. None would offer a comfortable ride.

To reach the river mouth 'as big as the Thames at Woolwich' the
Englishmen had to row across 'as much sea as between Dover and

Calais' in stormy weather, 'the wind and current being both very strong'. They had a native pilot, known to them as Ferdinando, but it soon became apparent that he would be little help: 'he was utterly ignorant, for he had not seen [the Orinoco] in twelve years, at which time he was very young, and of no judgement'. They quickly got lost in a 'labyrinth of rivers'. Raleigh began to think, gloomily, that they could be there a year and still not find their way:

> For I know all the Earth doth not yield the like confluence of
> streams and branches, the one crossing the other so many
> times, and all so fair and large, and so like one to another, as
> no man can tell which to take: and if we went by the sun or
> compass, hoping thereby to go directly one way or other, yet
> that way we were also carried in a circle amongst multitudes
> of islands, and every island so bordered with high trees as no
> man could see any further than the breadth of the river, or
> length of the breach.

At last they stumbled upon a river, which they called the River of the Red Cross, thinking of *The Faerie Queen* by Raleigh's friend Edmund Spenser.

Seeing a canoe with three natives in it, they chased and caught it. They were being watched by 'the people on the banks, shadowed under the thick wood', but when it became apparent that Raleigh meant no harm, they became less hostile and offered to trade. Ferdinando went ashore to fetch some fruit and wine, and to meet the local lord. He took his brother with him.

However, the lord was angry with them for bringing strangers into his territory and ordered their death. Both brothers, independently of each other, slipped their captors' grasp. Ferdinando's brother was the faster of the two: he reached the creek and shouted that Ferdinando was about to be slain. Raleigh's men sprang into life and, seizing a native standing nearby – an old man, as it happened – they dragged him into the barge. They then threatened to behead him if they did not get their pilot back. He cried out to the natives on the shore, but they did not hear him. They were busy hunting Ferdinando in the woods with their dogs; the sound of the chase, the yelps and cries, echoed through the trees. Ferdinando, frantic, crashed through to the water's edge and climbed a tree; the Englishmen brought the barge about, and Ferdinando leapt down into the river and swam across, 'half-dead with fear'.

There was good fortune in this for Raleigh. They kept the old man as a pilot alongside Ferdinando: 'being natural of those rivers, we assured ourselves that he knew the way better than any stranger could'. Raleigh knew that they had been very lucky: 'but for this chance, I think we had never found the way either to Guiana or back to our ships'. The pilot must have felt rather more ambivalent.

Notwithstanding this encounter, Raleigh thought these people – the Tivitivas, as he called them – 'a very goodly people and very valiant, [with] the most manly speech and most deliberate that ever I heard of what nation soever'. The Orinoco in this region rises 30 feet between May and September. The Tivitivas, Raleigh says, lived on the ground for part of the year, but 'in the winter they dwell upon the trees, where they build very artificial towns and villages'. He was endlessly curious about the natives – about what they ate, if and how they farmed, how they lived – and, unusually for a European of his time, he was quick to praise and slow to judge.

The journey got no easier. Three days in and the galley was grounded, stuck so fast, says Raleigh, with grim humour, that 'we thought that even there our discovery had ended, and that we must have left four-score and ten of our men to have inhabited, like rooks upon trees, with those nations'. Eventually, stripping the boat of all dead weight, 'with tugging and hauling to and fro' they got it free. Not long after they found themselves far enough up river to have lost the benefit of the tide, and suddenly things became much harder. The current was formidable and they had no choice but to row against it or be flushed back out to sea. Again, Raleigh lied to his men. It would be but two or three days' work, he told them. However, everyone, even the gentlemen, took their turn at the oars, each for an hour's shift.

Three days went by and the men became desperate. The heat was intense and the river was lined with high trees blocking out the breeze; the current got stronger every day. Raleigh instructed the pilots to keep on lying: one more day, they were to tell the men, just one more day. They were approaching the equator and the temperature was rising. The pilots promised just four more reaches of the river. Then three. Then two. Then one. The food was dwindling, and there was nothing left to drink but the 'thick and troubled water of the river'.

'Wearied and scorched and doubtful', the Englishmen had nothing to do but to press on, 'to attain the land where we should be relieved of all we wanted'. As Raleigh points out, 'if we returned, we were sure to starve by the way, and the world would also laugh us to scorn'. There was some fruit to be snatched from the river banks and there were also

> birds of all colours, some carnation, some crimson, orange-tawny, purple, watchet [pale blue] and of all other sorts, both simple and mixed, [and] it was unto us a great good passing of the time to behold them, besides the relief we found by killing some store of them with our fowling-pieces.

Their old pilot now told them that, up a branch of the river, there was a town where they could get bread, wine, hens and fish. The galley would not pass, however. It was noon. The pilot said that they would be back by nightfall. Confident in his knowledge, they ate no food. After three hours they asked him where the town was: a little further, he said. Three more hours passed and the sun was setting. They began to smell betrayal. Night was almost upon them. Another four reaches, he said, and they rowed four and then four more: 'Our poor watermen, even heart-broken and tired, were ready to give up the ghost; for we had now come from the galley near forty miles.'

By now, the Englishmen were ready to hang the pilot, but, not knowing the way back, could not. Beneath the trees the night was black. The river was narrowing and they had to cut their way through the overhanging branches. They had not eaten since breakfast; hunger was gnawing at them, as was doubt. The 'poor old Indian' kept assuring them that it was 'but a little further, but this one turning and that turning'. At last, they saw a light and rowed towards it, hearing the village dogs barking. It was one o'clock in the morning. The lord of the town was absent, but they found all they wanted: bread, fish, 'Indian wine' and rest.

In the morning the men who had gone to the town for provisions returned to their anxious colleagues aboard the galley, who thought that they had been lost. The countryside was different here. Raleigh calls it 'the most beautiful country that ever mine eyes beheld'. It was a kind of Arcadia, with plains of lush, short-cropped grass, neat groves and deer drinking at the water's edge. There were plenty of alligators in the river too, and Raleigh claimed to lose a man to them, taken in full view of the boats.

The next day, back on the Orinoco, they met four canoes coming down the river. Two got away; the others pulled ashore, the men flying into the depths of the woods. Those that were taken were loaded with bread; one of those that got away, they discovered, had contained three Spaniards, one of them a refiner. Raleigh took some men to follow those that fled into the woods. Creeping through the bushes, he found a native basket that had been hidden. It was the refiner's basket: Raleigh recognized the quicksilver and saltpetre.

Raleigh offered £500 – a vast amount – to any man who could capture one of the Spaniards, but they could find only the natives who had piloted them. Raleigh kept one, named Martin, for his own pilot and, true to form, mined him for information about the Spaniards' gold and where they had found it. Equally true to form, he kept the knowledge to himself. They had not come to mine: they did not have the equipment, nor, says Raleigh, defensively, did they have the time. To fail to bring anyone with any knowledge or skill in ore extraction on an expedition intent on finding gold was beyond quixotic – and, indeed, beyond complacent. Frobisher had had such people on his voyages to Meta Incognita; Raleigh's half-brother Sir Humphrey Gilbert had had them too on his doomed voyage of 1583. Why didn't Raleigh? One suspects that he felt it beneath him.

For now, in any event, they had to keep moving: the flood of the river in spring demanded it. In his narrative Raleigh returns to the familiar theme that he had difficult choices to make in extraordinarily hard circumstances:

> Whosoever had seen or proved the fury of that river after it
> began to arise, and had been a month and odd days, as we
> were, from hearing aught from our ships, leaving them
> meanly manned 400 miles off, would perchance have turned
> somewhat sooner than we did, if all the mountains had been
> gold, or rich stones. And to say the truth, all the branches
> and small rivers which fell into [the Orinoco] were raised
> with such speed, as if we waded them over the shoes in the
> morning outward, we were covered to the shoulders
> homeward the very same day; and to stay to dig our gold with
> our nails, had been *opus laboris* but not *ingenii*.

Besides, he adds, with extraordinary *chutzpah*, he was shooting at another mark than mere short-term profit.

With a new pilot on board, Raleigh dispatched Ferdinando and the old man back to the coast with a letter for the ships. The new pilot had been told by the Spanish that the English would eat him or 'put him to some cruel death'. He was pleased to find that this was not the case.

They were now 15 days into their journey of discovery. By rights they should have been back at their ships by now. Every extra day risked disaster. Yet it was only now that progress seems to have been made, for they could see the mountains of Guiana and there was a fresh, strong northerly wind to bring them on. They landed for the night on a sandbank, where they found turtles' eggs by the thousand. It was 'very wholesome meat, and greatly restoring,' Raleigh recalls, and his men, happy with the food and the sight of their goal, were content at last.

The next morning they were visited by the local lord, Toparimaca, together with three dozen or so of his followers. The natives brought fruit, wine, bread, fish and meat, and they feasted together. Raleigh had some Spanish wine; it went down well. Less circumspect than before, he consulted Toparimaca about his next move for Guiana.

Toparimaca brought them back to his village, Arowocai, which Raleigh found delightful: 'it stands on a little hill, in an excellent prospect, with goodly gardens a mile compass round about it, and two very fair and large ponds of excellent fish adjoining'. It could have been in England.

Some of Raleigh's men sampled the local wine, which made them, he says, 'reasonable pleasant'. There were two other *caciques* here and the wife of one of them caught Raleigh's eye:

> That *cacique* that was a stranger had his wife staying at the port where we anchored, and in all my life I have seldom seen a better favoured woman. She was of good stature, with black eyes, fat of body, of an excellent countenance, her hair almost as long as herself, tied up again in pretty knots; and it seemed she stood not in that awe of her husband as the rest, for she spake and discoursed, and drank among the gentlemen and captains, and was very pleasant, knowing her own comeliness, and taking great pride therein. I have seen a lady in England so like to her, as, but for the difference of colour, I would have sworn might have been the same.

Toparimaca provided Raleigh with yet another pilot, who proved his worth immediately. The river was now anything up to 20 miles across, 'with wonderful eddies and strong currents, many great islands, and divers shoals, and many dangerous rocks'. When the wind blew the galley threatened to capsize. Now when they stopped for the night they sought out the islands and sandy banks where the turtles laid their eggs.

In a couple of days they reached the port of Morequito and anchored there. They sought an audience with the king, for whom the Spanish were the enemy, since Berrio's men had slain his nephew. He arrived the next day, having walked the 14 miles from his house. He was, says Raleigh without a hint of incredulity, 110 years old. He walked back the same day. There was plenty of food again, brought freely by the villagers, including a novelty, pineapples, which Raleigh, greatly impressed, calls 'princess of fruits that grow under the sun'. South America seems to have been softening him. His guard was down more and more; he became increasingly generous in his judgements and less sceptical. This was not necessarily a good thing. One of the villagers gave Raleigh an armadillo, which he studied carefully and describes in his book, but it was of course the king he most wanted to see. His name was Topiawari. Raleigh came almost to revere him. To begin with, Raleigh used the same speech he had made at the coast: the Queen had commanded him to 'undertake the voyage for their defence, and to deliver them from the tyranny of the Spaniards'. To some extent Raleigh knew that this was just the expedient line to take; but part of him believed it, too.

Naturally, the conversation soon turned to Guiana. Raleigh realized that here, in Topiawari's realm, he was finally close to his goal. Raleigh asked the king about the people who lived on the other side of the mountains. Topiawari told him that in his father's lifetime, when he himself was young, a nation had come down into the valley of Guiana from the west – 'from so far off as the sun slept' were the words Topiawari used. They wore red and there were too many of them to be resisted. They had slaughtered many of the ancient peoples of the area, as many as there were leaves in the wood upon all the trees, and now they were lords of all. They built a city on their borders, called Macureguarai, at the foot of the mountain where the great plains of Guiana began. It was close by, just four days' travel from where they were sitting. In the last battle Topiawari's eldest son had been killed with all his friends and followers. Topiawari sighed a great sigh, says Raleigh, 'as a man which had inward feeling of the loss of his country and liberty, especially for that his eldest son was slain in a battle on that side of the mountains, whom he most entirely loved'.

The next day Raleigh pressed on to meet the peoples who lived to the west along the Caroli River, who Topiawari had told him were deadly enemies to these invaders. Raleigh's party came to the mouth of the Caroli early the following morning, hearing the roar of waterfalls before they saw them. They had aimed to row some 40 miles up river, but were unable 'with a barge of eight oars to row one stone's cast in an hour'. They pitched up by the side of the river and Raleigh dispatched various groups, some to make contact with the natives, others to search for minerals. He himself took ten or so men to see the waterfalls, 'every one as high over the other as a church tower, which fell with [such] fury, that the rebound of water made it seem as if it had been all covered over with a great shower of rain'. In some places, he says, they 'took it at the first for a smoke that had risen over some great town'.

Raleigh was now keen to go back, perhaps feeling his age. 'For mine own part I was well persuaded from thence to have returned, being a very ill footman,' he says. Yet when the others drew him on, little by little, he was grateful that they did so:

> I never saw a more beautiful country, nor more lively
> prospects; hills so raised here and there over the valleys; the
> river winding into divers branches; the plains adjoining
> without bush or stubble, all fair green grass; the ground of
> hard sand, easy to march on, either for horse or foot; the deer
> crossing in every path; the birds towards the evening singing
> on every tree with a thousand several tunes; cranes and
> herons of white, crimson and carnation, perching in the
> river's side; the air fresh with a gentle easterly wind; and
> every stone that we stooped to take up promised either gold
> or silver by his complexion.

They had nothing but their daggers and fingers with which to tear at the rocks, but they did what they could. None of them really knew what they were looking for. Although Raleigh liked to give the impression that he was always in the know, his knowledge was amateur and unproven. His men, meanwhile, were being seduced by fool's gold, to Raleigh's evident chagrin. If such stones had been brought back to England on his ships, he says in his book, that is no reason to judge El Dorado a fraud:

> it shall be found a weak policy in me, either to betray myself
> or my country with imaginations; neither am I so far in love
> with that lodging, watching, care, peril, diseases, ill savours,

bad fare, and many other mischiefs that accompany these voyages, as to woo myself again into any of them, were I not assured that the sun covereth not so much riches in any part of the Earth.

There seemed to be promises of wealth everywhere. There was a lake not far away that, when it sank every summer, revealed great quantities of gold dust on its shores. Topiawari's people told their visitors of a crystal mountain, which Raleigh himself saw in the distance when journeying home. But for the length of the way and the season of the year, he would have attempted to reach it (there was always a reason why he returned home empty-handed):

We saw it afar off, and it appeared like a white church-tower of an exceeding height. There falleth over it a mighty river which toucheth no part of the side of the mountain, but rusheth over the top of it, and falleth to the ground with so terrible a noise and clamour, as if a thousand great bells were knocked one against another. I think there is not in the world so strange an overfall, nor so wonderful to behold.

There were, he heard, diamonds and other precious stones on the mountain, which could be seen shining from very far off.

Raleigh seems to have begun to believe everything he heard by this point. Near the Caroli, he says, there was 'a nation of people whose heads appear not above their shoulders'. This may be thought a mere fable,

yet for mine own part I am resolved it is true, because every child in the provinces of Aromaia and Canuri affirms the same... They are reported to have their eyes in their shoulders, and their mouths in the middle of their breasts, and that a long train of hair groweth backward between their shoulders. The son of Topiawari, which I brought with me into England, told me that they were the most mighty men of all the land, and use bows, arrows and clubs thrice as big as any of Guiana... And farther, when I seemed to doubt of it, he told me that it was no wonder among them; but that they were as great a nation and as common as any other in all the provinces, and had of late years slain many hundreds of his father's people, and of other nations their neighbours... For mine own part I saw them not, but I am resolved that so many people did not all combine or forethink to make the report.

It's hard to see how he could have thought such stories would advance his cause. Perhaps, though, it was symbolic, since this was as far into Guiana as they would go. All that lay beyond blurred into fantasy, the stuff of dreams. Raleigh's ambition was swollen like the river in spring; he was no longer fighting the current, but was riding it back downstream.

It was, Raleigh suggests, the river that defeated them – that, and the season. El Dorado, he thought, was just a few days' march away, almost within his sights. Yet it is never quite clear from his account where precisely the tipping point was, the moment at which he decided that they couldn't go on to conquest. It must have been here, at the furthest limit of their leash:

I thought it time lost to linger any longer in that place, especially for that the fury of [the Orinoco] began daily to threaten us with dangers in our return. For no half day passed but the river began to rage and overflow very fearfully, and the rains came down in terrible showers, and gusts in great abundance; and withal our men began to cry out for want of shift, for no man had place to bestow any other apparel than that which he ware on his back, and that was thoroughly washed on his body for the most part ten times in one day; and we had now been well near a month every day passing to the westward farther and farther from our ships. We therefore turned towards the east.

The going back was swift. Against the wind they travelled 100 miles a day. Raleigh revisited Topiawari, wishing to talk seriously with him about Manoa and how to take it. On Raleigh's instructions he and the old man were left alone in his tent, save for an interpreter. Topiawari told him that it would be foolish to attempt a conquest now. Raleigh had probably already decided against it anyway, but having someone else to underwrite his decision was helpful, lest anyone think him weak, or foolish, or dishonest. The time of year was wrong, too, Topiawari said bluntly, and Raleigh had too few men. If they proceeded they were sure to end up being buried there. Moreover, he would need to build alliances with the native tribes; without their help, for food and guides, it would be impossible. A Spanish force of 300 had tried it, or so Topiawari said: but the people of Manoa had surrounded them on the plain and set the long dry grass on fire, so that the Spaniards were suffocated, gasping for air, too weak to fight, the smoke blinding them to their enemies. Macureguarai itself could be taken, with the forces at Raleigh's disposal, but Raleigh was unsure about the quality of his men and the quantity of his ammunition. He thought, one implies, that it all would have been easier than this. Raleigh and his men conferred, but he had made up his mind:

> We fell into consideration whether it had been of better advice to have entered Macureguarai, and to have begun a war upon [Manoa] at this time, yea, or no, if the time of the year and all things else had sorted. For mine own part, as we were not able to march it for the rivers, neither had any such strength as was requisite, and durst not abide the coming of the winter, or to tarry any longer from our ships, I thought it were evil counsel to have attempted it at that time, although the desire for gold will answer many objections. But it would have been, in mine opinion, an utter overthrow to the enterprise, if the same should be hereafter by her Majesty attempted. For then, whereas now they have heard we were enemies to the Spaniards and were sent by her Majesty to relieve them, they would as good cheap have joined with the Spaniards at our return, as to have yielded unto us, when

they had proved that we came both for one errand, and that both sought but to sack and spoil them.

Topiawari asked for some men to protect him from the Spanish, but Raleigh could spare none, at least none whom he could trust to be left behind. Topiawari offered Raleigh his only son to take back to England and Raleigh left two men in his stead. One, Francis Sparry, wished to stay; he was charged with travelling to Macureguarai and on to Manoa, if he could. Another, a boy named Hugh Goodwin, was to learn the language of Topiawari's people.

As Raleigh and his men sped back down river, they became increasingly fearful. The nights were stormy and dark, full of thunder and great showers, and the days were no better. The force of the current terrified them as much as the rage of the weather and by now the boats, which had never been spruce, were disgusting. The men had been

driven to lie in the rain and weather in the open air –
without shift, lying most sluttishly – in the burning sun, and
upon the hard boards [of the boats, which were also used to]
dress our meat… Wherewith they were so pestered and
unsavoury, that what with victuals being most fish, with the
wet clothes of so many men thrust together and the heat of
the sun, I will undertake there was never any prison in
England that could be found more unsavoury and loathsome,
especially to myself, who had for many years before been
dieted and cared for in a sort far more differing.

It was on reaching the river's mouth that they became most afraid: 'then grew our greatest doubt, and the bitterest of all our journey forepassed; for I protest before God, that we were in a most desperate estate'. There was a mighty storm and the men in the galley had to fight for their lives. The more Raleigh dithered, the worse things got. Eventually he decided that they would try the crossing to Trinidad, now that they were 'all very sober and melancholy, one faintly cheering another to shew courage'. They found their ships at last: as Raleigh says, there 'was never to us a more joyful sight'.

Raleigh had little to show for his efforts, but El Dorado was now in his blood. He spent the next 20 years of his troubled life plotting to get there.

The Courtier's Son's Tale

Raleigh's last best dream turns sour

As Raleigh no doubt expected, his *Discovery* and the news it contained could hardly be said to have had an unmixed exception. Among the poets, his friends leapt to his defence. Spenser, Marston and Chapman weighed in, although the last two must have been at least a little ambivalent, considering the going-over that they and Jonson – not, as far as we know, close to the Raleigh family at this point – would give to loose-tongued sailors in their play *Eastward Ho* a few years later. Chapman, in particular, wrote a long poem on the subject of Guiana, which included such lines as these:

Riches and conquest and renown I sing,
Guiana, whose rich feet are mines of gold,
Whose forehead knocks against the roof of stars,
Stands on her tip-toes at fair England looking,
Kissing her hand, bowing her mighty breast...

Shakespeare sat on the fence. In *The Merry Wives of Windsor* he makes Falstaff – not, it's true, most people's idea of a man with integrity – compare Mistress Page to 'a region in Guiana, all gold and bounty'. That could cut either way. But in *Have with You to Saffron Walden* Thomas Nashe has a character pulling out his purse and saying that he will 'change some odd pieces of old English for new coin; but it is no matter, upon the return from Guiana, the valuation of them may alter,' which sounds – as one might expect from someone of Nashe's contrarian instincts – rather like sarcasm.

That is nothing compared to the tongue-lashing that Raleigh received from the poet Joseph Hall, who in *Virgidemiarum* (1598) dismissed him as no better than a bumpkin:

Venturous Fortunio his farm hath sold
And gads to Guiane land to fish for gold
Meeting perhaps if Orenoque deny
Some straggling pinnace of Polonian rye.

Despite the snarling, the carping and the laughter, Raleigh never abandoned his dream of El Dorado. It represented everything he needed and wanted: renewed wealth and power, royal favour, a chance to bloody the nose of Catholic Spain. Indeed, just four months after Raleigh returned from Guiana he sent his redoubtable and brilliant lieutenant Lawrence Keymis back there. Keymis's brief was to open a mine at Caroni, where Raleigh and his men had scrabbled for gold in the dirt. Raleigh may, perhaps, have privately doubted the existence of the golden city, but he seems never to have doubted that there was gold to be found somewhere in the north-eastern corner of South America.

Keymis, however, brought back bad news: Berrio had built a

Spanish town, named San Tomé, at Morequito and Topiawari, its aged king whom Raleigh had revered, had been slain. No doubt, in part, this was recompense for having entertained 'Guaterrale', a reminder to the natives not to be so forgetful of Spanish power next time round. No doubt, too, Raleigh recalled that Topiawari had asked for 50 Englishmen to stay in Morequito to guard against such reprisals and that he had said no. Yet there was no point now in dwelling on Topiawari's prescience: he had predicted that death would take those who went into Manoa unprepared, as it had taken his own son, 'whom he most entirely loved'. Even if men could be got past San Tomé, Keymis reported, the Spanish had stationed men at Caroni, too. Nevertheless, there was some consolation for Raleigh: his name and his promise of liberty were still remembered on the Orinoco, with kindness and with hope.

Raleigh continued to finance expeditions to the region. Indeed, he regarded it as territory in which, now that he had claimed it for England, the Spanish were interlopers. The Spanish, naturally, demurred from this position, which would have mattered rather less if James I, after his accession to the English throne in 1603, hadn't shifted foreign policy towards an accord with Spain.

If Raleigh had entertained hopes that his fortunes would be revived under the new monarch, he was quickly and brutally disabused. By the end of 1603 he had been convicted of plotting James's overthrow – ironically, in collusion with the Spanish – and was lucky to escape execution. He spent the next 12 years in the Tower of London. He was released in 1616, with James's approval, to lead an expedition to conquer Manoa. His conviction – and the attendant death sentence – still hung over his head, however.

This was, to say the least, one last bold throw of the dice for Raleigh, the more so, because the terms under which he sailed were impossible to comply with. James wanted Raleigh to avoid any conflict with the Spanish, yet he was to sail with 1,000 men into territory that Spain had both claimed and garrisoned. The Spanish, not unreasonably, regarded this as something close to a declaration of war.

It doesn't add up now and it didn't add up at the time. The court was awash with rumours: Raleigh intended to turn pirate; he planned to build a kingdom of his own; he was in the pay of France; he would seize the Spanish treasure fleet sailing out of the River Plate. Perhaps he did consider all these possibilities. Sir Francis Bacon, for instance, claimed that Raleigh had floated the last idea to him in conversation. On Bacon's response that it would be piracy, Raleigh allegedly laughed and said that no one was a 'pirate for millions'.[1]

In any event, Raleigh sailed from Plymouth with 14 ships on 12 June 1616. His flagship was the *Destiny*. Financing the expedition had been tough; among the contributions was £2,500 from his wife, Bess, who had sold her estate to raise the money.

On the voyage across the ocean the crews of all 14 ships were ravaged with illness. Raleigh lost 42 men that way – not that he cared greatly. He thought that many of the men were the 'scum of the Earth' and, imperious and proud as always, he did little to hide his contempt for them. He himself was sick, too. He was, after all, in his sixties now, an old man by the standards of his time. He could eat nothing but stewed prunes, and those rarely; he was racked with fever, changing his sweat-soaked clothes several times a day. He drank day and night. He collapsed on deck, hitting his head.

In other words, Raleigh was unfit to lead the expedition up the Orinoco and passed the responsibility to Keymis. Raleigh would stay down at the coast, fretful and expectant. Keymis set out up the river on 10 December, with some 250 men, among them Raleigh's beloved but impetuous 22-year-old son Wat. Soon they arrived within sight of San Tomé, where Raleigh had talked with Topiawari more than 20 years before. Shortly before noon they disembarked and approached the wooden palisades of the town.

The lengthy preparations and politicking back in England had exacted their price. Whatever the Spanish thought Raleigh's actual motives were, his intentions in the short term had been abundantly clear for months. The men at San Tomé were accordingly well-prepared. They ambushed Keymis's men and there was a running battle.

1. It should be said that Bacon isn't that reliable as a witness. A sometime friend of Raleigh's, he was also instrumental in reviving the prosecution of Raleigh – and specifically the death sentence – after his return.

The English stormed the town. Wat Raleigh, wild as he was, leapt ahead of his soldiers, scenting glory, shouting above the clamour. He was silenced instantly, shot in the throat. It was a wasteful and need-less loss, some thought, among them Keymis and one of his captains, who later wrote, with a soldier's disdain for gentleman amateurs, that Wat had 'lost himself with his unadvised daringness'. The town fell around 1 am the following day.

News of the battle reached Raleigh on 13 February 1617. Keymis himself, having abandoned the attempt to hold San Tomé, led his men back on 2 March, having, it seems, searched for an open Spanish mine, rather than the new mine that he and Raleigh believed to exist. His men openly despised him – a judgement he seems to have shared. One of his captains wrote later:

> at last we found his delays mere illusions and himself a mere Machiavel, for he was false to all men and odious to himself, for most ungodly he butchered himself, loathing to live since he could do no more villainy.

Keymis must have known the reception that would await him back on board the *Destiny*. He had served Raleigh with unfailing loy-alty for decades, but, with no gold and Spanish blood on his hands, he had brought his master to ruin. Then there was Raleigh's best-loved boy, dead in the ground at San Tomé.

When Keymis presented himself to Raleigh in his cabin, Raleigh would not hear him out. Keymis begged him to accept his apology and his defence for not proceeding on to Caroli as planned, but Raleigh replied that, 'seeing my son was lost, I cared not if he had lost a hundred more in opening the mine, so my credit had been saved'. He added, coldly, that Keymis 'had undone me by his obsti-nacy, and that I would not favour or colour in any sort his former folly'. Keymis, too, suddenly turned cold: 'I know then, sir, what course to take.' Raleigh read nothing into that remark; he probably barely heard it.

Keymis went back to his own chamber close-by. Raleigh heard a shot and sent a cabin boy to investigate. Keymis was propped up on the bed, unharmed. He had discharged a pistol out of the window, he said, to clear it. A short while later, though, Keymis was found dead, lying as he had been minutes before but now with 'much blood by him'. The boy, turning him over, 'found a long knife in his body, all but the handle'. The gun was still by his side; he had shot himself, but the bullet had shattered a rib and gone no further. The knife was through his heart.

Raleigh knew that the only thing that could redeem him now was gold. Keymis had at least brought some gold ingots out of San Tomé, along with documents referring to nearby mines. Raleigh made immediate plans to return up the Orinoco. 'I would have left my body at St Thomé by my son's,' he wrote, 'or have brought with me out of that or other mines so much gold ore as should have satisfied the king that I had propounded no vain thing.'

Everything was unravelling now: Raleigh was old and ill, desperate, broken with grief and love for his son, fearing for himself, as well as for his wife and her future. His men could sense his confidence ebbing, and with it his authority. He was tainted with the prospect of ruin, and they wanted no part of his plans. With the Spanish fleet approaching, they refused even to stay where they were.

By 12 March Raleigh's ships were at Nevis in the Leeward Islands. They began to melt away, slipping away among the islands after nightfall, and there was nothing he could do to stop them. Events were pulling hard against him as the expedition fell from his grasp. As his options narrowed new plans emerged, spinning out wildly from his exhausted mind: he would sail to Newfoundland and take on supplies, then return to Guiana; he would get a commission from France; he would take the Spanish treasure fleet after all...

In the midst of this chaos, on 22 March, he wrote to his wife Bess, for the first time on this voyage, laying bare the loss of their son:

I was loath to write because I knew not how to comfort you.
God knows, I never knew what sorrow meant till now.
Comfort your heart, dear Bess, I shall sorrow for us both...
My brains are broken and 'tis a torment to me to write, and especially of misery... If I live to return, resolve yourself that

it is the care for you that hath strengthened my heart... I live
yet and have told you why.

Perhaps he had put off writing, hoping for better news to balance
the bad. None would ever come.

Postscript

The language of ice

We consider vocabulary

It is almost impossible to exaggerate the extent to which those seafarers who ventured west from Europe in the early modern period were sailing into the unknown. It wasn't simply the lands and peoples of which they were ignorant; there was also the sea.

The first seacharts – often called portolans – were no more than instructions on how to sail from one harbour to another, marking winds and tides, rocks and channels, where they were known. But, self-evidently, the distances across the Atlantic were of a different order to those involved in crossing, say, the Mediterranean. And in any event, there were no ports on the other side and harbours were not exactly easy to locate. Most voyage narratives at some point show the Europeans sailing up and down the coast trying to identify landmarks; in 1619-20 the Danish captain Jens Munk and his men endured a horrific and unplanned winter in Churchill Harbour, in Canada's northeast, because they lost their way and then became trapped by the ice.

In some ways, it is a measure of Sir Martin Frobisher's achievement as a sailor that he took three expeditions across the Atlantic in successive years, 1576-8, and reached the exact destination each time. But whatever the achievement was based on, it wasn't sophistication. The instruction to his ships if they got lost was to sail on latitude 77 until they got to Frisland and continue between 78 and 80 until they reached their destination. Then they were to shoot off guns to alert any other ships that might have made it already, and to light fires on the shore every night until the fleet was together. (Although this is not as rudimentary as the command, when lost in a fog bank, to make as much noise as possible with trumpets and drums.) Lines of latitude were less like guideropes and more like those that mountaineers use to secure themselves, and each other, to the mountainside; they were the last hope of safety.

And it wasn't merely the geography that presented new challenges; it was the climate too. For most of those Europeans who headed towards Newfoundland and points north, for example, the weather offered new terrors. It wasn't simply the cold, although one of Frobisher's men would complain bitterly that, 'here, in place of odoriferous and fragrant smells of sweet gums, and pleasant notes of musical birds, which other countries in more temperate zones do yield, we tasted the most boisterous Boreal blasts mixed with snow and hail in the months of June and July.'

It was the ice which awed them. The size of the icebergs, for men to whom a cathedral was almost the definition of vastness, was a visceral shock. The noises that the ice made, too, were unsettling – not merely the deafening crash of slabs falling away into the sea, but the ceaseless creaking and groaning. There was the way it moved around the ships with surprising speed, trapping the unlucky or unwary; or worse, the terrifying unpredictability of its movement and solidity underfoot for those compelled to cross it. It seemed to embody all the strangeness and instability of the new worlds into which these men had stumbled.

It is no wonder then, that seamen developed a large vocabulary to describe the varieties of ice they encountered as they battered against the Arctic Circle over the course of several centuries. Like the ice, the words and definitions were unstable, ever-changing, and usually unwritten. The following glossary, however, is culled from the unfortunate Sir John Ross's volume of 1819.

barrier	ice stretching from the land ice to the sea ice, or across a channel, so as to be impassable
bay ice	newly formed ice, having the colour of the water
beset	surrounded with ice, so as to be obliged to remain immovable
brash ice	ice in a broken state, and in such small pieces that the ship can easily force through
cake ice	ice formed in the early part of the same season
a calf	a piece of ice that breaks from the lower part of a field or berg and rises with violence to the surface of the water
field	a piece of ice so large that its extent cannot be seen
floe	a piece of ice of a considerable size, the extent of which can be distinguished
heavy ice	that which has a great depth in proportion and is not in a state of decay
hummocks of ice	lumps of ice thrown up by some pressure, or force, on a field or floe

iceberg	an insulated mountain of ice
land ice	ice attached to the shore within which there is no channel
lane, or vein	a narrow channel between two floes or fields
loose ice	a number of pieces near each other, but through which the ship can make way
nipt	caught and jammed between two pieces of ice
patch	a number of pieces of ice overlapping and joining one another
sailing ice	a number of pieces at a distance, sufficient for a ship to be able to beat to windward among them
sea ice	ice within which there is a separation from the land
stream	a number of pieces of ice joining each other in a ridge on any particular direction
a tongue	a piece projecting from the part of an iceberg that is under water

Bearers of gifts

The arrogance of some travellers is touched upon

I t is almost axiomatic that the Europeans took an absurdly patronising view of the kinds of gifts with which the friendship of Native Americans and other indigenous peoples could be bought. Consciously or otherwise, they seem to have viewed those they encountered as children, to be placated with brightly coloured ribbons and shiny toys.

It would be nice to take a revisionist line on this, but sadly the only actual list I have come across – again from the indefatigable Ross – rather bears out the traditional clichés. And seeing it in black and white makes, I think, the European mindset at that time seem yet more strange than anticipated – and more alarming. Specifically, these were gifts that he took on board ship from England in 1818, in the hope of winning the favour of the Inuit and other native peoples of Greenland and the parts of North America above the Arctic Circle. Sadly, the recipients' responses have not survived.

24 brass kettles
300 knives and forks in cases
20 felling and wedge axes
150 butchers' knives
150 yards of red flannel
100 yards of yellow flannel
100 yards of blue flannel
ten felling axes
200 looking glasses
2,000 Whitechapel needles
15 pounds of vermilion
36 cutlasses
1,500 gun flints
100 scarlet milled caps
14 swords
20 pounds of red thread
16 pistols
30 pairs of scissors
40 razors
50 coarse handkerchiefs
100 shoemakers' awls
35 rifles
2,500 balls for the rifles
102 pounds of snuff
four earthenware cases
150 pounds of soap
250 pikes
two hundredweight of iron hoops
129 gallons of English gin
129 gallons of brandy
13 cases of various beads and cowrie shells
40 umbrellas

It's an odd assortment, all in all. What does it say about English perceptions of the indigenous peoples of the Arctic? The first thing that leaps out is an apparent fondness for red. What factual basis this perception might ever have had is anyone's guess, but there can surely be little other sense in taking one and a half times as much red flannel as flannel of any other colour. And then, why only red thread, or scarlet milled caps, or vermilion dye?

Other gifts strike one as more than somewhat quirky. Just how practical, for instance, would umbrellas have been, so far north? Did the Inuit prefer brandy to gin? Was snuff popular in the genteel salons of the Arctic Circle?

And what exactly were they meant to do with all those iron hoops? If only we knew.

Provisions

Our attention is drawn to hunger

How men on Thomas Buts's ship could have been so desperate as to turn cannibal might be explained in part by this, more or less contemporary, list of provisions – mostly food and drink – which relates to a ship in the French navy with a crew of 60 being fitted out for an Atlantic voyage. It was the work of Antoine de Conflans, who later skippered Verrazzano's ship *La Dauphine*.

1,065 dozen pain biscuit (hard tack, in other words)
18 dozen fresh loaves of bread
One puncheon (two thirds of a hogshead) of flour
44 pipes (double hogsheads or tuns) of cider or beer
Two pipes of wine
Four pipes and one puncheon of salt meat
Half a carcass of fresh beef
Two fresh sheep

90 chests of lard
476 pounds of butter
One puncheon of peas
Half a pipe of beans
Six barrels of salt herring
160 pounds of candles
180 pounds of tallow
211 logs of wood
Half a pipe of vinegar
One barrel of verjuice (a liquor made from the unripe juice of apples or grapes)
Half a pipe of salt
12 pipes or barrels of water (which was, in fact, an afterthought).

The herring, butter, peas and beans were for fast days. The wine, fresh meat and bread were for officers only.

The End